GÜNTHER PFEIFFER

125 Years Steiff Company History

HEEL

HEEL Verlag GmbH
Gut Pottscheidt
D - 53639 Königswinter
Tel.: (+49) 22 23 92 30-0
Fax: (+49) 22 23 92 30-26
Email: info@heel-verlag.de
Website: www.heel-verlag.de

Under licence of:
Margarete Steiff GmbH, Giengen an der Brenz, 2005
Website: www.steiff.com

Author: Günther Pfeiffer, Taunusstein

Co-ordination: Marcus Reckewitz

Translation: Elizabeth Doerr

Copy-editing: Sharon Telfer

Typesetting and layout: Grafikbüro Schumacher, Königswinter

Lithography: GAF Günther Pfeiffer GmbH, Taunusstein
Website: www.gaf-pfeiffer.com

Cover design: Hess Medien, Syrgenstein
Cover photograph: Teddy bear 'Appolonia Margarete', 'Elefäntle' of
Anna Steiff and template of Margarete Steiff GmbH

Printed and processed by: Koelblin-Fortuna-Druck GmbH, Baden-
Baden

Printed and bound in Germany

ISBN 3-89880-535-2

GÜNTHER PFEIFFER

125 Years Steiff Company History

THE MARGARETE STEIFF GMBH

125 YEARS
1880–2005
MARGARETE STEIFF GMBH

HEEL

Contents

A look into Margarete Steiff GmbH's warehouse.

No. 80.

Fig. 1: Margarete Steiff,
a portrait by Otto Neubrand (1953).

Preface

**In 2005 Margarete Steiff GmbH
celebrates its 125th anniversary.**

The toy factory founded by Margarete Steiff in 1880 in Giengen an der Brenz developed from a small family-owned company into one of the most important firms for stuffed toy animals worldwide and has been able to retain its excellent market position to the present day. In the last 125 years, this company has not only decisively put its mark on the entire Ostalb region and Giengen, it has above all been of important influence on the design of children's rooms throughout almost the entire world.

Steiff creations from the early days of the company until well into the 1950s have become exceptionally sought-after antiques and collector's items. Record prices are regularly achieved at international auctions. For the last twenty years the current product range has also contained – alongside classic Steiff toys – special collector's editions, which enjoy great popularity.

The Steiff group, still owned by the family, but directed by Steiff Beteiligungsgesellschaft mbH, comprises among others Alligator Ventilfabrik GmbH and Steiff Förder- und Automatisierungstechnik GmbH, both also with their headquarters in Giengen an der Brenz.

One hundred and twenty-five years of Margarete Steiff GmbH – a good reason to retell the exciting and exceptional story of this company right from the beginning, a company that right up to today has stood, like no other, for tradition and progress, never forgetting its fellow men despite all its success.

Congratulations on 125 years of culture!

Günther Pfeiffer

'Button in Ear': A family and the story of its company

EYEWITNESSES AND

CONTEMPORARIES

MARGARETE STEIFF
GIENGEN A. BRENZ (W...

Erste Fabrik weichgestopfter Spie...
Marke: Knopf - im - Oh...

Leipzig: Zentralmessepalast :: Musterlager an 20 Han...
Fernruf 12 Telegr... ...renbrenz, Postscheckkon...

MARGARETE STEIFF G·M· GIENGEN A·/BRENZ
B·H· WÜRTTEMBERG

ERSTE FABRIK WEICHGESTOPFTER SPIELWAREN, MARKE „KNOPF IM OHR"
HOLZSPIELWAREN UND KINDERSPORT-FAHRZEUGE, MARKE „BÄRKOPF"

MARGARETE ST...

Firma

Fernsprecher No.12

Gienge...
MARGARETE STEIFF
Erste
Filzspielwarenfabrik
Deutschlands

Alleinfabrikation der ges.gesch.
Unzerbrechlichen,
leichten, starken, weichen
Stofftiere mit Eisengerippe
soliden Rädern & Stimen
600 NEUE hochfeine
Artikel!
Musterlager in Berlin,
Paris, Karlsruhe, Lei...
Überall grosse
Erfolg e. Expr...
nach alln Ländrn
Illustr. Liste gratis

Fol.

Fabrikation
von

Fig. 2: Beautifully designed stationery from Margarete Steiff's company –
forming the 'basis' of many contemporary documents of the company's history.

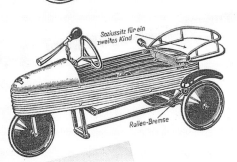

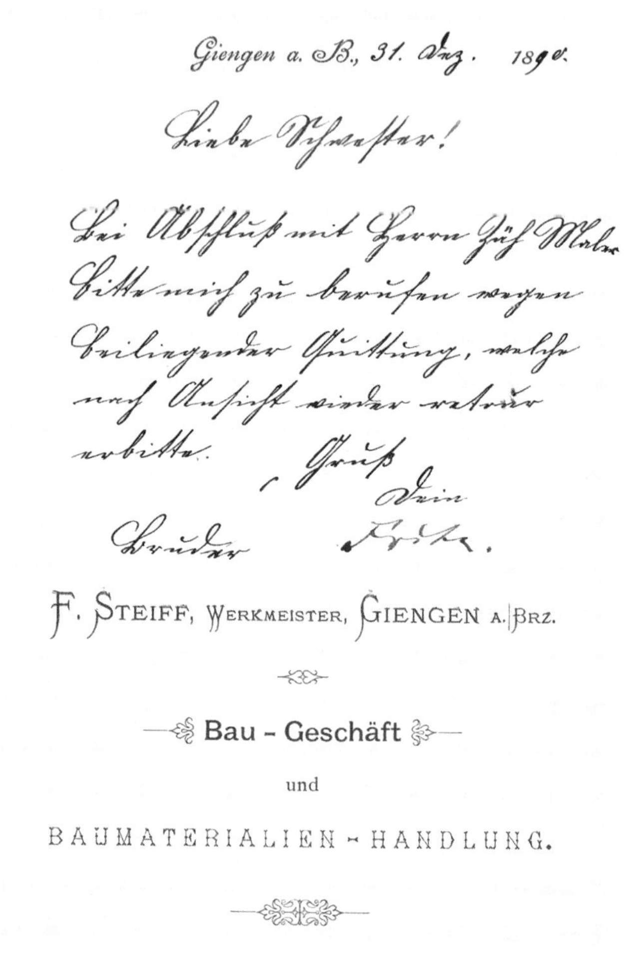

F. STEIFF, WERKMEISTER, GIENGEN A. BRZ.

—❦—

—❧ Bau - Geschäft ❧—

und

BAUMATERIALIEN – HANDLUNG.

—❦—

For the last 125 years toys have been manufactured in Giengen an der Brenz. In 1880 Margarete Steiff founded the company which is celebrating its 125th anniversary in 2005. This book tells of the company's history as well as its people. Naturally, there is no one left today who knew Margarete Steiff personally and could describe the events and details of her life.

The appeal of this publication honouring the company's 125th anniversary lies in tracing back the company's varied development right to the birth of its founder in 1847, depicting it as truthfully as possible. Facts are the order of the day, not hypotheses or speculations. Margarete's parents and siblings contributed greatly to the story of the factory's creation, above all her brother Friedrich, often called Fritz for short, as well as his nine children, the founder's nieces and nephews. So they take their place playing leading roles alongside Margarete Steiff. As the company's heirs, they determined decisive periods of the company's history, and so their lives also warrant close examination.

A popular saying states that the truth is rarely bent more often than at funerals and anniversaries. And like most such sayings, one cannot deny it contains some truth. For this reason, the history told on the following pages of Margarete Steiff's life and her company – one that has made millions of children and adults happy for the past 125 years with all of its beautiful toys – is always verified by contemporary evidence.

Fig. 3: A memo from Fritz Steiff to his sister Margarete from 31st August 1890.

10

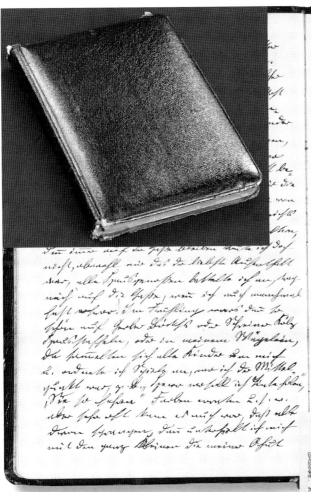

Fig. 4: A handwritten page from
Margarete Steiff's diary.

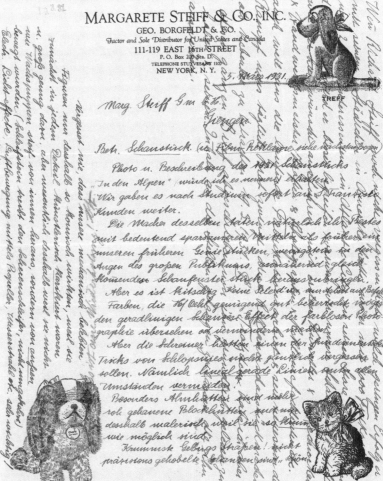

Fig. 5: A letter from Richard Steiff
from 5th March 1931. The margin
notes in red are commentary on
the content by Paul Steiff.

Fortunately there are a number of historical documents remaining in the Steiff company archives. Especially remarkable is the diary written in Margarete Steiff's own hand, which gives information from her earliest childhood all the way to the time of the toy factory's founding. Additionally there are numerous documents handwritten by Margarete and her brother Fritz Steiff as well as by her nephews, Paul, Richard, Franz, Hugo, Otto, and Ernst, all later managing directors of the company. There also remain many personal letters that Margarete Steiff wrote to her nieces Lina, Eva, and Maria.

A company policy strongly driven by exports from the start meant trips abroad for leading employees. In addition, in 1923 Richard Steiff, the company's creative head, moved to the USA. This all led to a great deal of correspondence. And because at this time phone calls across the Atlantic were still very complicated and expensive, and avenues of communication that are a matter of course today such as fax and e-mail did not yet exist, letter-writing remained the only means of correspondence – something that is very useful for present-day research.

And last but not least, the Giengen City Archive houses an extensive collection of historic documents from the founding period of Margarete Steiff GmbH.

Friedhelm Steiff is of course a living contemporary who experienced at least part of the history himself and could provide reliable information about the period following World War II based on his own experiences.

Friedhelm Steiff is a great-nephew of Margarete Steiff. His father, Ernst Steiff, the youngest son of Margarete's brother Friedrich, was one of Friedrich's nine children to be designated heirs by Margarete Steiff.

Today another five family members with the same degree of relations to the company founder are still alive: two daughters and a son of Ernst Steiff, siblings of Friedhelm Steiff; a daughter of Hugo Steiff; and Richard Steiff's daughter, who lives in the USA.

Fig. 6: Friedhelm Steiff, born in 1934, was Managing Director of Margarete Steiff GmbH from 1970 to 1974 and has been Chairman of the Board of Steiff Beteiligungsgesellschaft mbH since 1995.

Friedhelm Steiff loves to think back to the time when his father told him and his three siblings stories of 'Aunt Gretle' and her nieces and nephews, his father's siblings. He knew three of his five uncles personally – Paul, Hugo and Otto – as well as their three sisters, Lina, Eva and Maria. Thoughts of his great-aunt Margarete Steiff still fill him with pride and admiration today:

> *Only in the last 15 years has it become clear to me what she built for our family, and what types of difficulties she needed to get past to do it. Earlier, my father told us children stories of Aunt Gretle. Today I feel a deep respect for the person, Margarete Steiff. It was her optimism and iron-willed energy in her work that gave purpose to the entire family.*
>
> *She had given up the basis of her livelihood until then – sewing clothing – and begun work on the toy factory. Turning away from the sewing workshop was a much bigger thing back then than today where everything is flexible. It was a gigantic decision, a basic about-turn from her daily routines. And all the while she had understood how to include her environment, her girls, her relatives, her nieces, and her nephews in a wonderful manner.*
>
> *For us descendants there is an obligation to retain and increase the capital which she left us, that is the Margarete Steiff GmbH. And we can best carry this through to the future by continuing to work according to Margarete Steiff's principles and style. We are now partners in the second, third, and fourth generations after the founder and must make sure that a fifth generation will participate intensely and with their whole hearts in the toy factory Margarete Steiff GmbH.*
>
> *I am proud to be a descendant of this wonderful woman and make every effort to fulfil the obligations this entails.*

Since the beginning, fulfilling obligations and modesty have not just been empty words for the Steiff family. They are inseparable from Margarete Steiff, and accompany the history of the company like a fine golden thread, running through the main reasons for the worldwide success and good reputation that have characterised Margarete Steiff GmbH until today.

Friedhelm Steiff especially enjoyed the time he was allowed to spend in the factory as a child.

Fig. 7: Margarete Steiff GmbH's 'Muzeibü'.
Friedhelm Steiff loved to spend time here
during his childhood.

Many of the days of my youth were spent there, in the east wing, the glass building, because that's where the prototype designers' offices were. The creation department – today it is called the design department – was called 'Muzeibü' for 'Musterzeichenbüro' according to our abbreviation enthusiast, Uncle Paul. And I went to Muzeibü after school and was allowed to watch them draw.

A childhood surrounded by Steiff toys, who wouldn't love to remember that? It is above all his information concerning the time from the 1930s, after the 50th anniversary of Margarete Steiff GmbH had passed, that are of great importance for the company chronicles. During his career, he was in the employ of Margarete Steiff GmbH for about ten years, between 1965 and 1974. He began as the director of sales, then this industrial businessman and mathematician took over direction of the computer department, finally entering the top management in 1970. More than 20 years ago he was one of those party to the decision to put Margarete Steiff GmbH into the hands of well-educated and experienced managers who did not come from the family's own ranks.

For me, the most important thing was the stability of the company's organisation regardless of further family differentiation. The point was to secure the inheritance of Margarete Steiff before it came to family feuds. We have learned from the negative experiences of other companies with similar backgrounds. I will cite an extreme case: a company was inherited by the two sons of its founder. In the family's third generation a hefty fight broke out between the two families. The dispute, which lasted for years, ended with the company being sawn in half. I said to myself: we're not going to have it like that! And that's why we took the path we did.

The fact that the family no longer has direct influence on daily business most certainly doesn't mean that our hearts don't continue to beat for the Teddy bears and donkeys and all the other wonderful products.

In 1981 Steiff Beteiligungsgesellschaft mbH was created, which has since represented the interests of all shareholders. From the first day, Friedhelm Steiff has been a member of the board, and until 1994 its Vice-Chairman. In 1995 he became the Chairman. Chapter 4, 'Opportunities and challenges', draws the most on information and company history originating from him.

How it all began ...

MARGARETE STEIFF'S PATH TO
SUCCESSFUL ENTREPRENEURSHIP

Fig. 8: Only a little elephant made of
felt, but since its inception, the world
has been a little more wonderful.

Generally it is great rulers, commanders, popes and other servants of God, artists, inventors, and discoverers who initiate fundamental change and advance the progress of mankind. Their names can be found in history books, and knowing them is a sign of a well-rounded education. Their words and deeds are often quoted by important and powerful people of the present day, on appropriate occasions – and those not so appropriate.

There is an additional number of people who have done just as many great things; their names, however, are found – if at all – exclusively in the fine print. They step into the spotlight only on very special occasions, and therefore mostly their efforts are recognised by only a small portion of mankind.

Appolonia Margarete Steiff, who founded the Steiff toy factory 125 years ago, belongs to this category of exceptional people noticed only after a second glance.

Fig. 9: Appolonia Margarete Steiff in her younger years.

Fig. 10: Giengen around 1830. The medieval city fortifications are easily recognised.

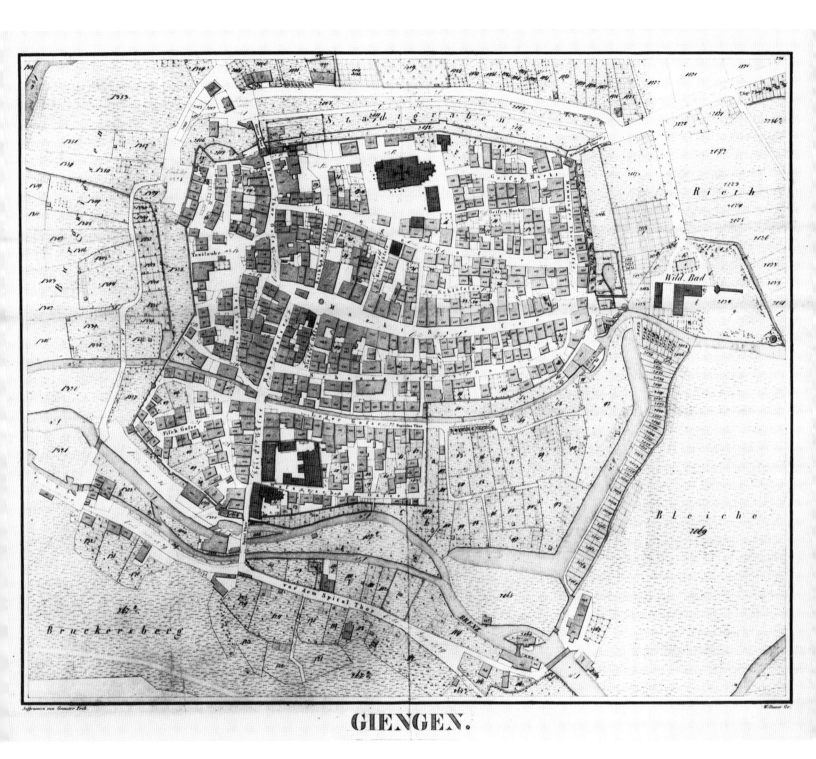

GIENGEN.

Fig. 11: A map of the city of

Giengen around 1830.

With extraordinary energy, she not only took control of her own life but also achieved great success developing a company with an exemplary, progressive philosophy. Above all, with her innovations and the toys she made, she revolutionised the paraphernalia to be found in a nursery at the end of the nineteenth century, contributing greatly to the fact that generations of children could finally have toys appropriate for their age. And, last but not least, she helped an entire region attain employment and prosperity. Nevertheless, she remained modest about these achievements throughout her entire life.

Fig. 12: Steiff toys from the nineteenth century.

STIRRING TIMES

Appolonia Margarete Steiff saw the light of day on 24th July 1847, in Giengen, located by the River Brenz in Germany. A former free city of the Holy Roman Empire, it is now part of the state of Württemberg, and lies north of Ulm at the edge of the mountainous Ostalb region. At this time it had little more than 2,000 inhabitants.

Her parents were Friedrich Steiff (born 28th July 1817), originally from Geislingen on the Steige River, and Maria Margarete (born 28th June 1815) from Giengen, daughter of Bartholomäus Hähnle and Anna Maria Hähnle (née Hodum). The two ran a construction business from their home on Lederstraße (then called Ledergasse) and already had two daughters, Marie (born 22nd February 1844) and Pauline (born 27th November 1845). Appolonia Hähnle, the sister of Maria Margarete Steiff, was Appolonia Margarete's godmother. So Margarete took her first name from her aunt; however, no one used this name in day-to-day conversation – friends and relatives all called the little girl either Margarete or by the affectionate abbreviation 'Gretle'.

With the birth of Friedrich on 27th December 1848 the family was complete. Friedrich was the only son and the youngest child, for Elisabeth – born seven years after Margarete to the day, on 24th July 1854 – died just a few days after her birth. Elisabeth's premature death was nothing extraordinary for the period. Infant mortality was very high in the mid-nineteenth century, and up to 50 per cent of newborns died within their first year.

Politically and economically, the times were anything but easy. The reactionary politics of many governments, coupled with social tensions, had led to revolutionary unrest throughout almost the whole of Europe in 1848. These events were triggered by the February Revolution in France. King Louis Philippe went into exile, and the Second Republic was established. In parts of the Austrian Empire and in Italy there were bloody uprisings, and in many regions of Germany a revolutionary mood ruled the day. Citizens and liberal politicians demanded German unity, a constitution and an all-German parliament.

Numerous conservative governments were being overthrown and replaced by liberal powers. After uprisings in Prussia, King Friedrich Wilhelm IV finally agreed to the completion of a German constitution and freedom of the press.

Fig. 13: The house where Margarete Steiff was born, Lederstraße 26.

Free elections to the National Assembly were agreed upon and were held on 1st May 1848. About 85 per cent of men were able to vote, but women were not allowed to. On 18th May, the first session of the National Assembly – the first freely elected, all-German parliament – was called to order in Frankfurt's St Paul's Church. It comprised 585 members, all men, who decided upon a democratic constitution. And, even though this set of basic laws was not fully implemented at that time, it was later used as a model for both the Weimar Republic's Constitution and the Basic Law of the Federal Republic of Germany.

All of this took place within Margarete Steiff's first year of life. These were stirring times – and, of course, they didn't leave Giengen untouched. Rumours of an invasion by the plundering and pillaging French triggered hysterical fear. Notwithstanding such terrible expectations, the region surrounding Giengen remained peaceful and life slowly returned to normal. And, despite her mother being pregnant during all this excitement and fear, Margarete's brother Friedrich was born without complications.

Fig. 14: Friedrich Steiff (1817-1894),
Margarete's father.

THE DIAGNOSIS: POLIO

Shortly after Friedrich's birth, the Steiff family suffered a dreadful stroke of fate. Margarete fell terribly ill. She could no longer walk: her left foot was completely paralysed and her right partially. Her right arm was also left extremely weak. Margarete had contracted poliomyelitis, or Polio as it is more commonly known. This was terrible news and a terrible illness.

Polio is highly contagious, an infectious disease passed by a virus. The infection is caught principally through ingesting contaminated food or drink, spreading in a similar way to Hepatitis A. After approximately one to two weeks, the illness makes itself known through unspecific symptoms such as headaches and muscle-aches, loss of appetite, diarrhoea, fever and difficulty with swallowing. After that, the pathogen forces its way into the central nervous system and triggers the second phase of the illness, which manifests itself with back pains, muscle-aches, and even meningitis and muscle paralysis. In the worst cases this can lead to permanent paralysis or even death.

And, until today, there has been no known specific treatment for Polio. One particularly prominent victim of this malicious disease was American President Franklin Delano Roosevelt (1882-1945); he fell ill in 1921 and subsequently was dependent on a wheelchair for the rest of his life. In 1952 the USA was plagued by a Polio epidemic. There were about 58,000 registered cases of Polio infection, and 3,145 of these people died. More than 21,000 people were left permanently paralysed in some way. In the same year, 9,728 cases of the illness were registered in the Federal Republic of Germany; 777 of these were fatal. Since 1960, however, the voluntary preventative vaccination that has been in use in industrialised countries has made the illness quite rare. A few drops of the vaccine are sprinkled onto a small cube of sugar and swallowed. It's that easy, these days.

During Margarete's time, however, one was pretty much at the disease's mercy without protection, something that would have serious effects for the young girl. Margarete's impressive account, written around 1908, demonstrates her incredibly sober assessment of the situation:

> At one and a half years of age, I fell ill and could no longer walk. My left foot was completely paralysed, my right foot partially, and my right arm was very weak. Otherwise I remained healthy from then on, and even did not have many of the other usual illnesses that children have.

23

Looking back, Margarete accepted what fate had dealt her; she didn't crumble from self-pity, but rather turned without dismay to the positive aspects of her childhood during the time that followed. This very pragmatic, down-to-earth woman kept a positive approach to life which she constantly reiterated and later expressed even more clearly.

Of course, her family did everything possible to help heal little Margarete's illness, or at least to alleviate the paralysis. But it is clear that this was no easy task at that time for a number of different reasons. Even the search for a suitable doctor turned out to be a hurdle. Many doctors were consulted, with the family often undertaking difficult journeys to do so. Here is another passage from Margarete Steiff's written memoirs:

> *Of course, we didn't pass a single opportunity by, and I can remember that my mother often took me to doctors in other towns. One time we went through Ulm, but for what reason I can no longer remember. There were no post carriages and trains back then. Once we had arrived, my mother asked some children to take me the rest of the way on their sled. Then we went to an inn called 'Gasthof zur Gans' where I was given a crisp fried sausage, and it's because of this sausage that the trip has stayed in my memory, for I no longer recall anything about the doctor we visited. ... On Whitsun 1856 my mother travelled with me to Ludwigsburg. ... At two o'clock in the morning we travelled by coach via Söhnstetten and Böhmenkirch to Süssen where the next train awaited us. I left my new hair ribbon in Söhnstetten, where we had a break. It had cost 12 kreutzer and was made by Lotte Mesner. I never again received anything so beautiful. In Ludwigsburg I was fortunate to be taken in by Dr. Werner's family and felt at home there. I enjoyed more freedom there than I did at home. So I did not miss my home at all. I also often visited the children's nursing home. Dr. Werner put a great deal of effort into healing me. He made two tendon cuts on my left foot. A plaster cast was supposed to make my foot straight again, but since all signs of strength were missing, the following treatment in Wildbad did not take the desired effect. ... It was really very nice at the Herrnhilfe in Wildbad* [AUTHOR'S NOTE: THE CHILDREN'S CLINIC OF PEDIATRICIAN DR AUGUST HERMANN WERNER, 1808-1882, LOCATED IN THE BLACK FOREST]. *There was a quite lenient administrator there who let me go into the attic all by myself and slide around in the garden. I didn't care how my clothes looked. I played hide-and-seek with the others. ... There were not many other children there who were unable to walk at all like me. However, they all had much worse illnesses than me, and were sometimes in a great deal of pain, so that I was the healthiest of all.*

Fig. 15: 'Herrnhilfe', located in the spa resort Wildbad, where Margarete Steiff stayed several times.

Fig. 16 left: Margarete Steiff was dependant on a wheelchair all her life.

Again, there is not a word of complaint to be found here about the difficult journeys, the pain following the operations, or even her own disability. On the contrary, she uses the smallest opportunity to find something positive, an attitude toward life that deserves deep respect. But despite her unbroken optimism and all the efforts and expenses: Margarete Steiff will be dependent on a wheelchair all her life to get around.

AN ALMOST HAPPY CHILDHOOD

Although the effects of the polio severely restricted her daily life, Margarete experienced a comparatively happy youth. She didn't withdraw into herself, she was sociable, and she was very popular with everyone. In her *Memoirs of Miss Margarete Steiff,* written almost one hundred years ago, she makes the following observations:

> *I visited my grandparents a lot, for I couldn't stay outside all the time, even if that was my favourite place to be. I begged all the others in the house to carry me outside, even if sometimes I almost froze. … In the spring it was so wonderful on the front steps of Schreiner Kölz's or Gerber Böckh's house or in my little wagon. All the children gathered round me and I arranged the games so that I was in the middle of them. … But often they all ran off to play, and then I talked to the really little ones that were entrusted to my care. I always had room for two or three of them in my little wagon, and our neighbour was always happy when I took care of her children.*

Inarguably, Margarete's greatest – and, because of her disability, certainly quite risky – adventures were the two occasions in her childhood when she almost drowned:

> *One time the attendants were pulling us a bit too fast outside of the yard, an there was a pretty deep puddle with dirty water. The wagon fell over and we children, eight to ten of us, fell head over heels into the water. I had a calliper on my foot and sunk right down to the bottom, following the law of gravity. Since help was right there, all we had was a good scare. We were put straight to bed and got sweets from everyone and for a few days we were the most important people in Wildbad.*
>
> *It seems incredible that I actually fell into the water twice. The first time I was maybe four years old and my three siblings and I were allowed to go to the field with our lovely old neighbour, Jesaias Edelmann. While he was mowing, I was put on the edge and given some flowers to play with while the others helped our neighbour or played around. On the way home, he put us all on top of the mown clover in the cart. Back then, the Brenz's shoreline along Ledergasse was still quite rough. Our neighbour had to move over to avoid hitting another horse and cart, came too close to the bank, and the cart with all four children tipped over into the water. My sister Pauline was completely buried underneath the clover. But since there were a lot of people right there, we were soon fished out.*

Fig. 17 above:

Margarete Steiff's diary.

Fig. 18 below: An excerpt from

Margarete Steiff's handwritten entries.

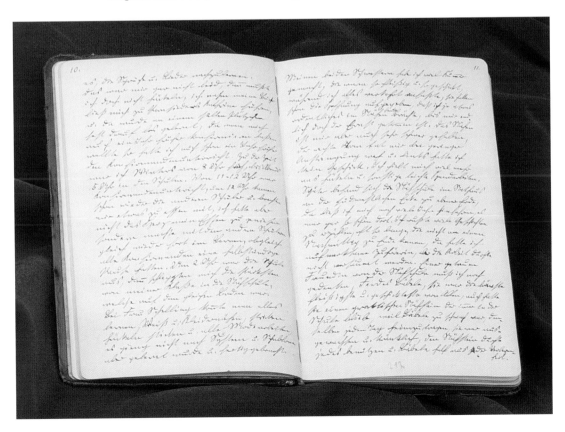

Fig. 19: One of Margarete Steiff's dolls,
wearing felt clothes she made herself.

Fig. 20: A wagon pulled by two cows brought in crops for the farmers.

Almost 60 years after this incident, Margarete still remembered every detail. There was, however, not a trace of fear in her account:

> *I can still remember that my apron was up over my face and I saw the design of the carnations against the black background. When I was asked what I would have done if I had not been fished out, I answered that I would have swum to my aunt at the Klingen Mill. I can't remember having been afraid or scared.*

Looked at from today's point of view, it's a great stroke of luck that Margarete Steiff wrote down the story of her life only about a year before her death. It's not so much the description of historical events that are important. These are far more extensively and better documented in many other sources. It's much more the smaller, daily occurrences that she recounts. Her nature and her character reveal themselves far more impressively in these stories than in any other place.

SCHOOL AND OTHER OBLIGATIONS

It is not just leisure time and pleasure which determine a childhood, there are also obligations. As well as watching smaller children as mentioned above, Margarete had to do crochet work. This was an occupation that she didn't like at all. She tried to use every other task she was entrusted with to avoid this despised activity:

> *Our neighbour was happy when I watched the children. For me it was also an important task because I didn't need to crochet during that time, for usually I had to have a certain amount of it to be done. ... Because of the two summers I spent in Ludwigsburg*

Fig. 21: Even for healthy children living was not easy in the nineteenth century.

and Wildbad, I had fallen behind at school. Therefore I had to learn the missed school-work and songs. That was not bad at all, for then I didn't have to crochet.

Already as a child, Margarete analysed things critically. She didn't just accept things as they were without protest; she had her own ideas and her own will. This becomes especially clear in the following lines:

I had to fight for myself, for my mother was a determined enemy of pleasure and rest. Those words just weren't in her dictionary, only work, work, and work again.
Today I am of course grateful from the bottom of my heart that she taught us to work hard and to have an undemanding nature, and that she didn't spoil me as mothers often spoil and nurse afflicted children.
I was never as good and obedient as my sisters, and I was often called 'mean Gret'. One time as a school child, my mother was not at all satisfied with how much work I had done, even though I had been so industrious with the crocheting. I didn't touch any work for two days after that, saying if that's not enough then I won't do anything more at all. Naturally, that stopped very quickly, for my mother knew how to handle us.

This was an unusually energetic behaviour for a disabled girl who required constant assistance – and that at a time when, almost without exception, raising children meant disciplining them.

Of course, Margarete also had school and confirmation classes. She enjoyed both greatly, and she went at them with great seriousness and energy:

I really very much enjoyed going to school and was not deterred by foul weather, although I could have easily obtained leave. … Since I was to have my confirmation a

Fig. 22: Giengen's city hall. Margarete Steiff
went to the sewing school here for many years.

year early, I began taking confirmation classes a year earlier as well. During that time I was at the schools from eight o'clock in the morning until five in the evening in the winter. From 11 am to 12 noon I was in confirmation class, and at noon the other students came already, bringing with them something for me to eat. I didn't have the heart to enjoy my food, however, but immediately continued lessons with the others even though all of the confirmation candidates had a half-hour break.

Her way to school seems to have been – almost – perfectly organised:

My siblings or the children next door took me with them. Near the school a woman was entrusted with the task of carrying me up the steps. Not infrequently my team just left me in front of the school to hurry into their classrooms. But Mr Schnapper was there to take care of me. The teachers also often carried me back and forth.

31

Fig. 23: Early felt work done by Margarete Steiff.

At the same time Margarete was also attending sewing school. The tasks given her there were not easy for her at the beginning, since her right arm was so weak and her left was so untalented.

> At 2 pm school was out, and then the strongest from my class carried me to the sewing school, which was on the same floor.
> Mrs Schelling was able to teach us everything: to sew linens and clothes, knitting, crocheting, needlepoint, and fashion work. There was no system or patterns, but we learned and completed the work.
> Both my sisters were quite worried about me: they were so industrious and talented, while I had two left hands so to speak. They had given up hope that I would ever be able to sew something well, until I finally got serious about it. I found sewing really difficult. My right arm hurt with even the smallest amount of effort, and my left arm had no skill. ... Later the sewing school was located in the city hall at the south-west corner on the ground floor. I continued going there for many years because it was so very nice there.

Upon reaching her confirmation, Margarete's school days had also almost come to an end. Around 1860, regardless of how talented and gifted they may have been, girls could not attend secondary schools. The knowledge they needed to fit into their given roles as wives and mothers was transmitted to them in primary and sewing schools. Many girls worked after school for a while for others of high standing and then married at a relatively young age. Thus, the livelihoods of the young women were seen as secure. The tasks allotted to them comprised running the house and bringing up the children.

Margarete's older sisters, Pauline and Marie, had already left their parents' house at this point and were in service to others. Only her younger brother Fritz stayed at home until he transferred to building school:

> *My sister Marie, who was good in school and was very industrious and obedient, took a position as a nanny for the wife of Chief County Judge Bazing in Neresheim after her confirmation. ... The year before, my sister Pauline was confirmed and she soon went to our aunt. She was there for a while, after which the preacher's wife organized her a position in Augsburg where her knowledge of sewing was put to good use. After a few years, she went to Mrs Hartmann's spinning mill in Heidenheim as a chambermaid. ... Now, only my brother Fritz remained at home. He was loyal to me and I took part in his studies. ... Then Fritz went off to building school and I was alone with my parents.*

Her parents were very worried about what would become of their disabled daughter. Who would take care of her when they were no longer there? And, naturally, this is something Margarete could feel:

> *That was a hard time for my dear mother because she worried so much about my future. ... When my sisters had gone, my dear mother had to take care of the housework, much of the business, and me. Often, it was too much for her, especially when her feet were sore. ... My mother suffered much from her bad feet, then she got very upset, especially since she had to wait on me and refused to accept any help.*

When both of her sisters had gone, Margarete Steiff used every opportunity possible to bring some variety into her life. Girls from the neighbourhood took care of her and helped bring some distraction into her rather monotonous daily routine during these years. Margarete was very grateful for these friendships:

> *Although my sisters had gone, I did not become lonely, the neighbours' daughters and friends were very loyal to me. My mother would have liked to see me go to bed*

at 7 pm in the summer because she needed to rest her aching feet. I did not agree with this, however, so my friends picked me up to take me on a moonlight walk. Afterwards the girls put me to bed, and closed the front door behind them. So I had been taken care of and had been able to get some air after the perpetual sitting around in the room.

One of Margarete's deep desires became fulfilled: she was allowed to begin learning the zither. Thus, with the music she was able to compensate somehow for the social contacts otherwise missed due to her disability. In the memoirs which she recorded much later in life, the joy she felt as a child is still discernible:

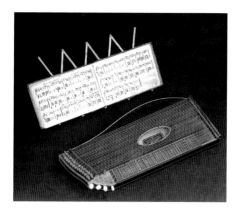

Fig. 24: Playing the zither was one of Margarete Steiff's great joys.

> *Finally, my deepest desire was fulfilled. I was allowed to learn the zither. … Mr Sautter, an old musician who owed my father something, gave me lessons and my friend Mr Ranz, who was very musical, helped me keeping the time. Only much later I did buy myself a zither method book and then learned it thoroughly, also gave lessons.*

Alongside the social aspects, Margarete found more advantages in playing the zither: by giving zither lessons she not only earned some money, but she also trained the fingers of her right hand, something that also helped in her sewing work.

ON THE ROAD TO INDEPENDENCE

Margarete Steiff finally gave up all hope of being cured when she reached the age of eighteen. After innumerable doctors' visits, operations, health cure treatments and periods staying in clinics she determined the following for herself:

> *… but my limbs had not improved in the least. I searched for healing for a long time until I finally said to myself, God has determined this for me, that I can't walk, therefore it has to be all right this way.*
> *From then on, at about 17 to 18 years old, I no longer became excited about any extolled medicine or healing methods, for a pointless search for healing won't allow one to find peace.*

Margarete accepted her disability without a trace of resignation, of complaint about the hopelessness of her situation, or of depression – clear and sober thoughts determined her decision about the future.

Already in her younger years, Margarete Steiff's entire course of action was characterised by an exceptional determination. And she well understood how to do the work she was able to do, despite her disability, to the advantage of everyone.

Of course, she also worked to earn money, but money was not her main priority. For as well as income, above all work guaranteed happiness and variety for her.

Fig. 25: Giengen around 1866. The city fortifications came down little by little.

Margarete could communicate, she could laugh with others, and she could make music, leading an almost normal life. She was often hired by her customers. One can assume that she was already working regularly by this time.

At the time my sisters had left, I visited my Aunt Appolonia often and helped quite a bit with the marriage settlements for Hähnle's sons. For many weeks I had to clean feathers with an old Memmingen woman and didn't go home all week because I slept there, earning at least 42 kreutzer per week plus food. My earnings of course improved as my performance did. Later I was allowed to cross-stitch names. ... When the preparations for the settlements of Michael, Melchior, Hans, and Georg were done, we began on Christine's dowry. We sat for many months in the upper room, where we worked and sang. ... After I was no longer needful there, the wife of Gross, the city clergyman, discovered me. Enterprising as she was, she had me brought to her every day and I helped her with the dowry for her daughter, Tusnelde. It was totally new for me to be working with a family completely outside our own, and I enjoyed it and the stimulus it brought to me.

Additionally, I was teaching zither and therefore needed to be at home on certain days. ... Teaching the zither paid a little more than handicraft work.

Over the time Margarete earned herself a small stockpile of money with this type of work. When her sisters came home, they joined forces. Luckily the children didn't need to give their parents any of the money they saved and could thus continue to save kreutzer by kreutzer.

We children were allowed to keep every kreutzer, and slowly but surely our little piles of savings grew. We kept our spending to a minimum.

In the time that followed, they made quick progress with their joint efforts. It wasn't long before their "piles of savings" helped them to buy a practical new object: a sewing machine. This was the first sewing machine ever in Giengen an der Brenz!

The sewing machine was invented in 1790 when Englishman Thomas Saint registered a patent for the sewing apparatus he had invented. During the years to follow many inventive spirits occupied themselves with its technical development, but only in 1846 did American Elias Howe manage to design a truly usable machine with a double stitch to create a machined seam. Nowadays famous names such as Isaak Merrit Singer and Allen Benjamin Wilson entered the scene somewhat later and in connection with further technical progress.

Fig. 26: Margarete Steiff owned the first sewing machine in Giengen an der Brenz.

Margarete and her sisters Pauline and Marie now owned one of these modern machines. And, of course, they were very proud of their new purchase, attacking new tasks with great passion, something that ended less than comfortably for Pauline:

We had the first sewing machine here, and now we wanted to work in a strict manner. We had a lot to do during festivity periods and often heard Jonathan or Ensle call out midnight or our bell announce the late hour with two strikes. At one Pentecost we went to bed at 6 am. Sister Marie couldn't stay up that long, so she got up earlier and took care of the housework. All that sewing and working didn't hurt me at all, but Pauline ruined her health with it.

For Margarete's siblings, it was soon time to start thinking about marrying. Pauline married Fritz Röck in 1870 and Marie wed Michael Häussler in 1873. In the following year, her brother Fritz married Anna Böckh. After all the other siblings had left their parents' house, Margarete began to worry more and more about how she would continue to be in control of her own life. But her positive attitude toward life and her sociability soon helped her out of this crisis:

When Pauline married in 1870, Marie in 1873, and Fritz in 1874, I was a little scared about what would become of me. But I had no need to be; I was never lacking helpful friends.

Fig. 27: Margarete Steiff was a beautiful young woman. Her handicap is not visible at all on this picture.

In 1870-1871, France and the German states finally went to war. And even Giengen's residents were drafted to serve, among them Adolf Glatz, husband-to-be of Marie Hähnle, the daughter of Margarete's Aunt Appolonia. Margarete took good care of her cousin, who was of course greatly worried about her future husband:

> *When, in 1870, Marie Hähnle's fiancé, Adolf Glatz, had to go to war, I remained most of the time with the bride-to-be who was left behind.*

Fortunately the war did not last long. On 1st September 1870 the decisive battle was fought near Sedan. Napoleon III and his army surrendered to the Germans, who continued on to Paris. The city finally capitulated in January 1871. The peace treaty signed on 18th May 1871 in Frankfurt am Main ended the war between France and Germany. For Germany, the end of the successful war coincided with the states' unification under Prussian leadership. On 18th January 1871 the Prussian King, Wilhelm I, was crowned German Kaiser (Emperor) in the Hall of Mirrors of Versailles – so, through his persistent efforts, Bismarck finally attained his goal of the unification of Germany.

And, at last, the soldiers returned. In Giengen the joy was great:

> *When, after this frightening time, the troops came back home, there was much joy, especially for the bride-to-be. A happy time followed for the joyous couple. ... In the autumn of 1871 the double wedding of Hans and Lina Hähnle and Adolf Glatz and Marie Hähnle took place.*

Margarete continued to work diligently during the war and after it. She extended her list of clients and had meanwhile begun to sew modern clothes. Despite her very disabled right arm, she used the sewing machine perfectly by employing a simple trick:

> *The number of my customers had gradually increased to quite many. I also had to make modern clothes. I learned this by helping Christine Brandstätter with relatives, and little by little I was able to work independently, although I never liked it. I loved to make children's clothes. Soon I had the opportunity to do this for families I was friendly with.*
> *In the meantime I had also discovered that I could operate a sewing machine with my left hand by putting it in front of me the wrong way around. That was a great breakthrough.*

And she loved to travel. Since at the time, there were no special facilities for disabled people, everything needed to be well planned and prepared. But even

Fig. 28: The Brenz River flows directly alongside the houses on Lederstraße.

when something went wrong, such as when the post wasn't delivered punctually and as a result no one was in place to welcome her, Margarete knew how to help herself. This talent for improvisation was certainly one of her great strengths – giving up on a planned goal because of an unplanned circumstance was not part of her character. 'Giving up is not in my dictionary,' is probably how she commented on such situations. Thus, over the years, she travelled to Geislingen, Neckarsulm, Stuttgart, Ludwigsburg, Augsburg and Lindau, among others. Many of her trips were undertaken alone even if she preferred to travel in company. She loved to remember those times and reported extensively on her occurrences and experiences:

> *By my love of travel, I clearly illustrated the truth of the saying 'People love to do precisely things which they can't do very well'. My first trip took me to Geislingen. ... The second trip was with Adolf Glatz and his young wife to Neckarsulm. ... From there, I travelled alone to Stuttgart and, since my letter hadn't arrived in time, I was not picked up. I called a porter who took me to Mrs Vollherbst. She was completely horrified when I arrived so totally unexpected. ... One time I was also in Ludwigsburg visiting the city clergyman's wife Mrs Gross. From there we went on an excursion to Monrepos* [AUTHOR'S NOTE: CASTLE MONREPOS ON LAKE EGLOSHEIM] *and I even took a boat trip on the lake. ... I visited my siblings in Augsburg twice.*

Margarete especially enjoyed her contact with the Glatz family:

> *I had become good friends with the very lovable Glatz family. They were completely different people from those I was used to in our family, which was so full of cares and work, hardly able to enjoy life. There in Neckarsulm it was wonderfully cosy and this visit remained one of my favourite memories.*

Adolf Glatz, husband of Margarete's cousin Marie, had meanwhile become the business partner of his brother-in-law Hans Hähnle. Margarete excitedly followed the founding activities of the company Württembergische Woll-Filz-Manufaktur Giengen (entered onto Heidenheim's registry of companies on 14th March 1866) through reports given by her Aunt Appolonia:

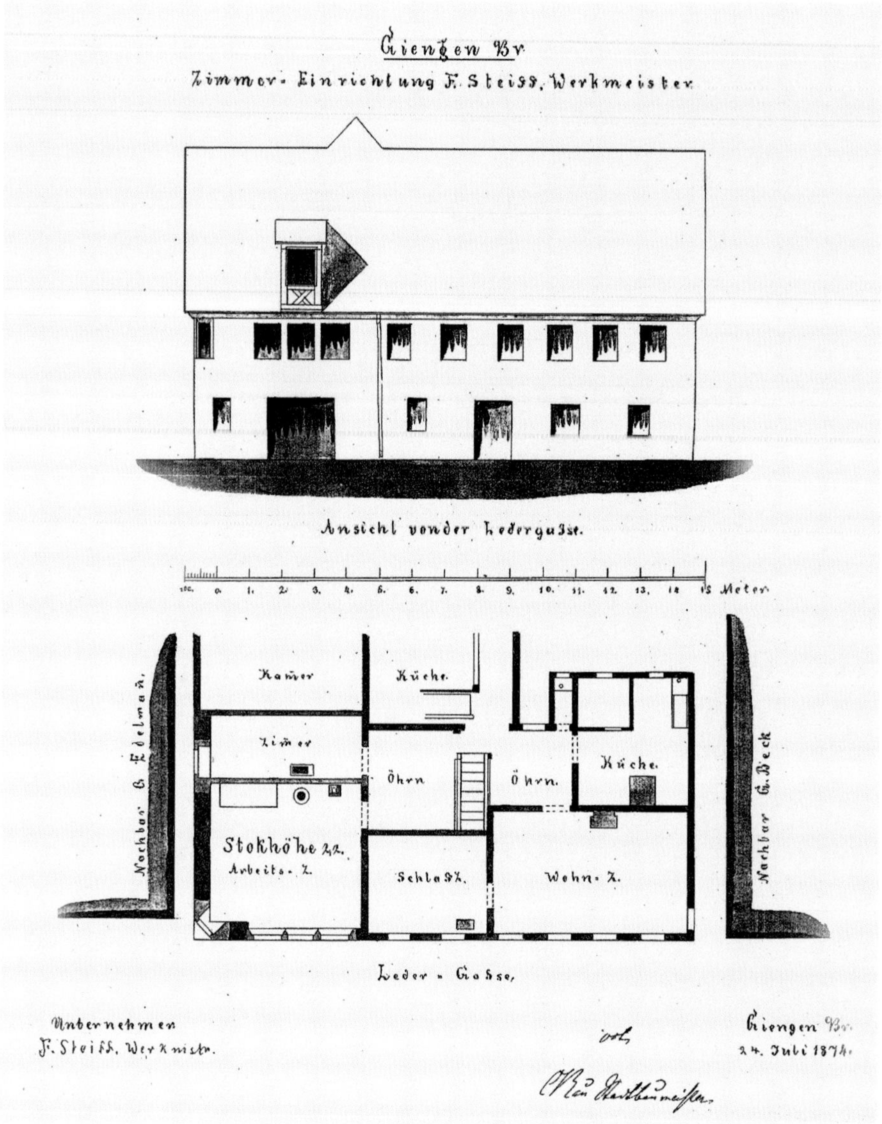

> *From the creation of the felt factory, I felt tied to it in a very personal way. My Aunt Appolonia, who was quite excited about the foundation of the business, always told us of her worries and battles concerning it. It was a difficult beginning that almost overstretched the financial resources of the Hähnle family, but with tough endurance and untiring diligence the result was finally gained.*

Adolf Glatz was to play a decisive role in the establishment of Margarete Steiff's business just a few years later. But first there were great changes in the Steiff family home. Margarete's father planned a conversion of his house in 1874. Blueprints dated 24th July 1874 – Margarete's twenty-seventh birthday – show her own apartment within her parents' house and, even more important, her first workshop. After the reconstruction was finished, she set up her first real tailor's workshop on the first floor of the house on Lederstraße. This building was renovated in recent years by Steiff Beteiligungsgesellschaft mbH and was turned into a museum, the 'Margarete Steiff Geburtshaus' (Margarete Steiff's Birthplace), which has

Fig. 29: Blueprints from 24th July 1874 for the conversion of Margarete's Steiff's parents' house.

been open to visitors since November 2003. Also her workshop was largely brought to its original state and is now partially equipped with tools that belonged to the family (see page 164).

A BUSINESS CONCEPT MADE OF FELT

In 1877 it was Adolf Glatz who advised her to open a ready-to-wear felt shop. The manufacture of felt was already at a relatively high technical level at the time, and the material was even quite suitable for making clothes. The establishment of the felt shop was a large step for Margarete Steiff, but the savings she had from her small sewing business made it possible for her to take the risk, especially since she trusted Adolf Glatz as an expert adviser and good friend at her side; he was also the source of excellent and extensive contacts due to his position at the Württembergische Woll-Filz-Manufaktur. She wrote the following of this period in her memoirs:

> *Felt was becoming ever more perfect and could be used for clothing. In 1877, when I had some savings from all my various handwork, with the help and assistance of Adolf Glatz I took the risk of opening my own ready-to-wear felt shop. At first I only produced wares for Siegle, a commercial textile shop in Stuttgart.*

Her courage and readiness to take a risk were rewarded. The shop did well from the beginning, and in the first year she was already able to hire several employees. The girl who had caught polio at a young age, who always required the physical assistance of others, had become a successful young woman who had taken control of her life despite her disability – and is truly loving it. Instead of being resigned to it, she embraced her fate. At only 30 years of age, she had founded her own business and become an entrepreneur. Quite remarkable, and even more so when one thinks about how difficult something like this must have been during the second half of the nineteenth century for a woman – and especially a disabled one. Margarete, on the other hand, describes her success soberly and modestly as usual with few words:

> *My business did well right away in the first year and I was able to employ several people. But I couldn't give up sewing clothes myself for I would have made my dear friends and relatives much too unhappy if I didn't make their clothing and dress their children.*

41

The following two years were also very satisfying both professionally and personally. Margarete Steiff still had close contact with her siblings. Therefore, when her sister Marie died in 1879 while giving birth to her third child, it hit her very hard. But her positive attitude toward life, her talent for accepting things she could not change, and even retaining her courage in the darkest hours all helped her to overcome this painful loss. Thus in the same breath she remembers not only the death of her sister but also the recovery of Marie's oldest daughter Emilie, who survived a terrible illness. If Margarete Steiff ever made the conscious decision to take care of her siblings and their children for life, then it was probably finally made at this moment:

Marie was a very active businesswoman, and besides continued to sew. Unfortunately she died in 1879 during the birth of her third child, which was stillborn. That was a hard time for all of us. At the same time, her oldest child, four years in age, was very sick – even blind – with meningitis. Emilie soon recovered, though she had lost the sight in one of her eyes.

THE FIRST STEP IN BECOMING A WORLD-FAMOUS COMPANY – THE 'ELEFÄNTLE'

The year 1879, as well as being the year of Marie's unexpected death, was a truly fateful year for Margarete Steiff for a completely different reason. Like today, there were fashion magazines around at that time reporting on the newest trends and developments of prevailing taste. As a progressive and forward-looking entrepreneur, regularly reading these was of course obligatory for Margarete Steiff as well. In the magazine *Modenwelt* from 8th December 1879 she came across a pattern and directions for making a "cloth elephant as a toy". The original text to be used as directions read:

Fig. 30 left: The *Modenwelt* issue from 8th December 1879, featuring the instructions for 'cloth elephant as a toy'.

Fig. 31 right: Enlarged view of the elephant pattern from *Modenwelt*.

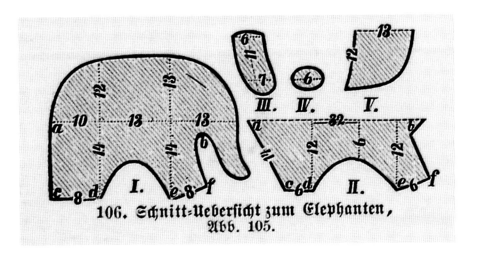

106. Schnitt-Ueberficht zum Elephanten,
Abb. 105.

Fig. 32: Felt elephant from the
period between 1892 and 1894.

Fig. 33: Gift to her sister-in-law Anna Steiff.
The initials AS are embroidered on the back
of the elephant.

Fig. 34: Enlarged view of the
elephant from *Modenwelt*.

Material: 67 centimetres of grey Futterbarchent [AUTHOR'S NOTE: A CLOTHING
MATERIAL MADE OF COTTON], *about one kilo of tow* [AUTHOR'S NOTE: HEMP AND/OR
FLAX SCRAPS], *one little piece of a colourful scarf or cashmere (for the saddlecloth); two
10 centimetre-long, white, bone knitting needles, two black porcelain buttons, colourful
silk. This is a pretty toy that will certainly be received with great joy by the little ones
and is not difficult for an aunt or a mother to make ...*

An exact description of the steps and the pattern followed. For Margarete, a skil-
ful seamstress, it was of course no problem to make this elephant. However, she
used felt instead of the recommended cotton material and fleece instead of tow for
the filling. In her memoirs she puts it like this:

44

Fig. 35: Two felt elephants from early Steiff production.

Fig. 36: Caricature elephants made of blue and red mohair plush, included in the Steiff range from 1909 to 1927.

At this point in time, a pattern for an elephant landed in my lap. Felt was very suitable for it and I filled it with the most wonderful fleece. Next I made presents of them to the children in the family and samples in varying sizes.

The 'Elefäntle' – or little elephant, as the first of Margarete Steiff's softly stuffed play animals was called – was first made only as a gift for children. At this time, Margarete had no idea what effect this little animal made of felt would have on her entire life. The last paragraph in her diary was consequently dedicated to this elephant. And once again the continuing close relationship she has with the Hähnle family becomes very clear.

Fig. 38: Elephants made of blue and grey mohair plush (1924).

Fig. 37: Velvet elephant pincushion (1927-1932).

Fig. 39: A seven-centimetre elephant made of mohair plush, felt blanket with the inscription '75 Years 1880 to 1955'.

Fig. 40: Anniversary elephant from 1930 with golden badge and imprint '1880-1930'.

Once I took a little elephant to the Hähnle family, where I still made children's clothes every now and then, and gave it to the present director as a reward if he could stop crying for the entire day, which, by the way, he always did extensively. But oh no, he couldn't contain himself, even when presented with the desirable elephant, and continued to cry. So I gave it to him anyway to quiet him again.

Records from the Margarete Steiff GmbH archives show that the first elephants of this type were sold in 1880. In December 1880, two were bought by Maria Spiess and another five by Lina Hähnle. This is the beginning of the toy factory and the present world-famous company, Margarete Steiff GmbH.

Fig. 41: Elephant made of Nomotta wool from the 1930s.

Fig. 42: Records in Paul Steiff's handwriting,

recording among other things the first sales

of elephants in December 1880.

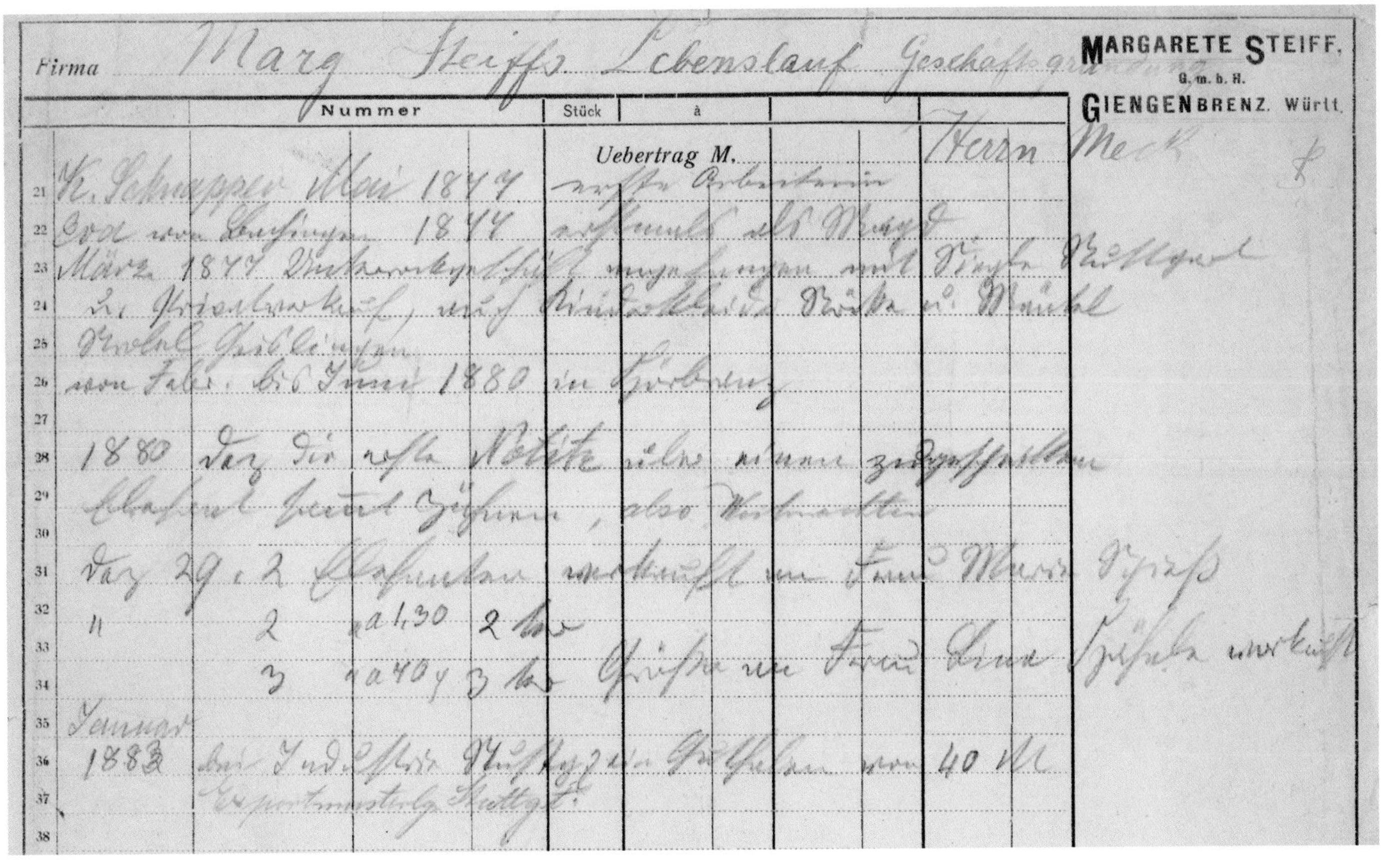

Fig. 43: Toy elephants made of curled wool plush (1934-1941).

47

III.
The family and the company

MARGARETE STEIFF AND

A CHANGE OF GENERATION

Fig. 44: The nine children of Friedrich Steiff. From left to right in the order of their age: Paul, Richard, Franz, Lina, Eva, Hugo, Otto, Maria and Ernst.

Toy manufacturing within Margarete Steiff's company began with the advent of the first little elephants, but of course the ready-to-wear felt clothing with which she still earned most of her money continued to take precedence. In the years 1880 and 1881 Margarete Steiff was still able to take the time to make longer trips. So, in February 1880, she visited the Glatz family in Hörbranz. Adolf Glatz had taken over the management of the Württembergische Woll-Filz-Manufaktur branch there. She was accompanied by her brother Friedrich during the trip and stayed until June of the same year as she later wrote in her memoirs:

> When the Glatz family was transferred to Hörbranz, I went to visit them in February of 1880 with my brother. Since Lake Constance had frozen solid the previous cold winter and no boat could pass, we travelled via Kempten and so on. That gave me the opportunity to see the mountains and the lake.

In 1881 she again visited the Glatz family, who had in the meantime moved to nearby Lindau. This was the last trip that Margarete Steiff reported in her memoirs:

> The next year I was allowed to go back and took part in the move to Lindau. I truly enjoyed everything during my time with the Glatz family; how wonderful were the cart rides around the lake!

She goes on to excuse herself in part for being absent so long from her business at home:

> At the time I did have a business at home where I made felt skirts. It wasn't that inflexible, however, and I could get away for a few months.

Even though she doesn't mention it at all, it is obvious that these trips were not only for pleasure. Judging by the ambition that Margarete displayed throughout her life, the time was certainly also used to talk about business and make plans. Perhaps even, during these days, the plans for the first catalogue (published in 1883) were made.

Unfortunately, when writing her memoirs, Margarete Steiff only covered the years up until 1881. There are, however, a number of other documents from the subsequent period still stored in Steiff's archives; Paul Steiff, above all, left behind extensive information with his numerous and detailed reports and stories. But it is hard for anything else to match the informative and honest words of Margarete Steiff.

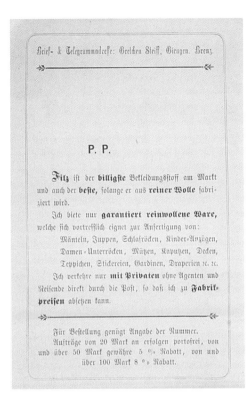

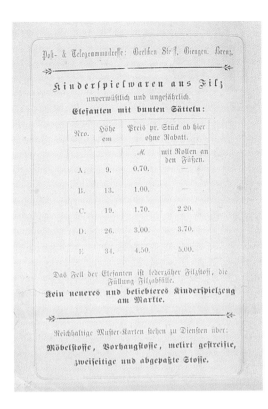

Fig. 47: The last page of the catalogue is reserved for toys made of felt.

Fig. 46: On this page Margarete Steiff gives instructions on how to work felt.

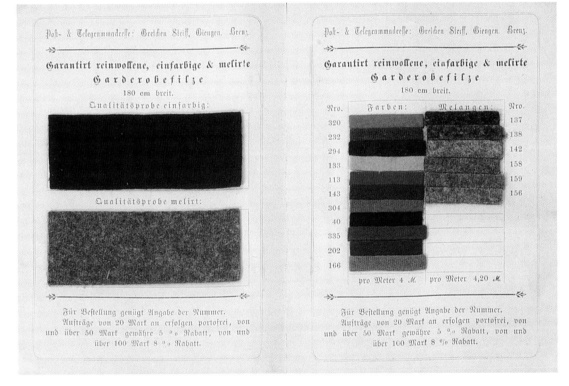

Fig. 48: Little pieces of felt glued into the catalogue serve as samples of quality and colour.

The above-mentioned catalogue from 1883 bore the title 'Price list of the felt mail-order business of Gretchen Steiff in Giengen a. Brz'. Her close co-operation with the Vereinigte Filzfabriken becomes especially clear in the following sentence, and also on the catalogue cover: "Guaranteed pure wool products of Vereinigte Filzfabriken".

Vereinigte Filzfabriken Giengen AG – as the complete name is written – evolved from the Württenbergische Woll-Filz-Manufaktur in 1881. The company, which belonged to Hans Hähnle and Adolf Glatz, had had a very successful business policy. Alongside the opening of various branches, in Hörbranz among others, factories were also bought up. In this way, over the years the company had earned its position as the market leader worldwide. It was turned into a joint-stock company, with Hans Hähnle taking over the position as president of the board. Adolf Glatz became the director in charge of the Vereinigte Filzfabriken and returned to Giengen with his wife Marie.

Felt products, therefore, are featured first and foremost in the catalogue. Toys are not mentioned until the last page, advertised as:

"Children's toys made of felt – unbreakable and safe – elephants with colourful saddles."

There were five different sizes offered – 9, 13, 19, 26, and 34 cm. The 19 cm version was also offered "with rollers on the feet". The catalogue went on:

"The skin of the elephant is a tough-as-leather felt material, the filling felt remnants. There is no newer or better loved toy on the market."

Margarete was launching the new product with a big fanfare. Interestingly, the wheeled version of the elephant is already being offered here.

THE TOY BECOMES SUCCESSFUL

The few commercially available toys until then were made of wood, stone, metal or porcelain – in other words hard materials. Margarete Steiff's elephant on the other hand had skin almost like fur and a soft filling. It was a toy designed to appeal to children, something that just asked to be cuddled.

From year to year the production of these soft, stuffed toy animals increased. A publication from 1930, commemorating the toy factory's fiftieth anniversary, supplies excellent and reliable information on this development and on many other events of the following years. The author of this account was Karl Vallendor, Steiff's advertising director in that anniversary year of 1930. Richard Steiff personally thanked Vallendor for his good and conscientious work on the chronicle with a personal, four-page letter from his home in Jackson, Michigan, USA.

The anniversary publication lists the exact number of animals produced up until 1890. According to this record, nothing but elephants was manufactured until 1885; these were made in small but ever-increasing numbers. Eight animals only were made in 1880, followed by 18 in the year 1881, 11 in 1882, 103 in 1883, 297 in 1884, and 596 elephants in 1885. The following year, 5,066 copies of the pachyderm were made and, for the first time, 104 monkeys were mentioned. So, from

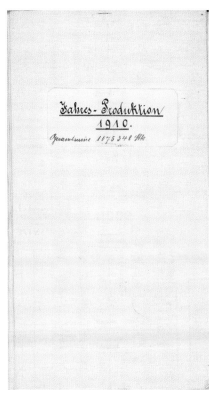

Fig. 50: Cover of the production list of 1910.

Fig. 51: Table from the 1930 anniversary publication with the pieces and numbers sold from 1880 to 1890.

Jahr	Gesamt	Elefant	Velo	Affen	Esel	Pferd	Kamel	Schwein	Maus	Hund	Katz	Has	Giraffe
1880	8	8											
1881	18	18											
1882	11	11											
1883	103	103											
1884	297	297											
1885	596	596											
1886	5170	5066		104									
1887	2686	2032		366	11	20	153	104					
1888	3997	2488	138	505	66	4	596	200					
1889	4682	2791	158	648			743	342					
1890	5480	1215	27	738	177	191	246	346	171	945	327	1088	9

Fig. 49: Cover of the 1930 anniversary publication '50 years of Steiff – 'Button in Ear'.

1886, a second type of animal was being made. In 1887 four new animals were added: donkey, horse, camel and pig. The total number of animals manufactured was 2,666 pieces. In 1888, the company produced 3,997 animals. And this time there was another novelty: 'Velo', as it was called, an animal sitting on a metal tricycle. In 1889, there were no further novelties but once again production increased, going up to 4,682 pieces. Finally, in 1890, the assortment grew to 13 different toy animals – including mouse, dog, cat, hare and giraffe – of which a total of 5,480 pieces were manufactured.

The anniversary publication contained more interesting information, such as the description of how the early rideable animals were made:

Strong wooden frames were made by a carpenter, each was swathed with felt, the skin pulled over it, and then the whole thing stuffed and the wheels added. The elephant – the first soft, stuffed animal on wheels – was accompanied by the donkey, horse, camel, pig, dog and giraffe, so that the collection was already quite colourful and varied just a few years after the first attempts.

Unfortunately, the numbers mentioned in the anniversary publication can no longer be followed in detail by looking at the original documents, since the publication mentions only the types of animals and not their sizes and possible differences in position or outfitting. Annual sales figures, in which the production numbers of all Steiff articles were recorded in detail, are only available from 1906. During this time Margarete Steiff still maintained a close relationship with her brother Friedrich (called Fritz for short). He also supported her in business matters and played rather a large part in the expansion of the company. It was his commitment that made the first wider successes with the small toy elephants possible. As the anniversary publication reported:

> *Master builder Fritz Steiff, the father of today's managing director and brother of the founder, had a great deal to do with the expansion of sales beyond the borders of Giengen. More than Margarete herself, he spotted the business opportunities of such 'playing around' and what it could mean. So, one fine day he took an entire sack full of the little elephants to a carnival in a nearby city where he proceeded to sell off weeks' worth of production. Then relationships with other businesses were forged, and in 1883 a delivery was reported as having gone to the export sample collection in Stuttgart.*

Fig. 52: A view of the planned residential and commercial house on the corner of Mühlstraße and Turmstraße from 1890.

CONSTRUCTION

In 1888 Friedrich Steiff took over his father's construction business. In Giengen he put up quite a few buildings; the renovation of the Gerschweiler paper factory, the construction of the felt factory in Hörbranz, and several edifices in Esslingen were also his work. In 1887 he bought the 'Pulverturm' tower from the city of Giengen, which he tore down two years later. In its stead he built a two-family dwelling, where Margarete housed both herself and her business.

This construction project was necessary, for the little atelier in her parents' house on Lederstraße no longer had enough room for Margarete and her enormously enlarged felt and toy production. The two-and-a-half storey house on the corner of Mühlstraße (today called Margarete-Steiff-Straße) and Turmstraße was built in 1890. The business was moved directly after the house was completed. The 1930 anniversary publication also has a passage covering this move; though its dating is out by one year:

> *In 1889 the business was moved from Lederstraße to Fritz Steiff's newly constructed edifice on Mühlstraße. A built-in shop with two large glass windows turned out to be very advantageous to the retail sale of felt, picture rugs, and toys.*

Friedrich Steiff had already built another almost identical house on Mühlstraße in 1888. This building, on the corner of Färberstraße, was the mirror image of the personal and business residence he built for Margarete Steiff two years later. However, it didn't contain a shop and served only as a home.

Fig. 53: The building erected in 1890 houses the 'Filz-Spielwaren-Fabrik' (felt toy factory).

Fig. 54: A view of Friedrich Steiff's construction project on the corner of Mühlstraße and Färberstraße, planned and built in 1888.

THE NEXT GENERATION

In December of 1889 Margarete Steiff's mother died. This was a heavy blow for the whole family, but especially for Margarete with her disability. Her mother had stood by her side every day for many years and took care of many things that Margarete was not able to do without assistance.

It was during this troubled time that Margarete's destiny appeared, in the person of Johanna Röck. The young sister-in-law of Margarete's sister Pauline, she lived in Heidenheim and visited often. In the 1958 biography of Margarete Steiff published by Calwer Publishing (Stuttgart), Elsbet Lange-Danielczick found the right words to describe the relationship between these two women. (Even she, however, like other authors, made mistakes in spelling the name and with the genealogical placement of Johanna Röck, which she spells Röckh: Johanna was not as is often thought the sister-in-law of Margarete's brother Friedrich, but of her sister Pauline). Lange-Danielczick writes:

Fate provided her with a companion. A sweet young sister-in-law of her brother often came to visit from Heidenheim: Johanna Röckh.

Johanna was drawn to Margarete. The workshop there was so interesting. How sunny the hours after work, and how festive every Sunday, with its flowers and songs, happy laughter, friends and children! Johanna had a delicate and impressionable disposition. But, under the guidance of such a mature, motherly friend, she recognised her task in life. She stayed with Margarete Steiff until the last hour of Margarete's life.

In Johanna Röckh, Margarete found her other half, both in work and play. Hers was not a nature created for loneliness.

When Margarete woke in the morning, the new day waited with many promises. Johanna came into the room and cared for the disabled woman with the joy of a young housewife, happy to be needed, to love and to care.

Fig. 55: Friedrich Steiff with the family's six sons. From left to right, front: Ernst, Hugo, Otto; left to right, back: Paul, father Friedrich Steiff, Richard, Franz.

So, in her personal life, Margarete Steiff was not alone. She had a companion at her side helping her to bear the heavy fate of her disability. This explains the way in which she took control of both her profession and her personal life, without any

Fig. 56: Mother Anna Steiff, née Böckh, with
the family's three daughters. From left to right:
Maria, Lina, mother Anna, Eva.

kind of inhibition – an unsatisfied and bitter person would not be able to accomplish such achievements.

But Margarete also had support within her family – a family that had grown through the years. A total of nine children, six sons and three daughters, were born between 1876 and 1890 of the marriage between her brother Friedrich and his wife Anna.

The oldest and first-born was Paul, born on 19th February 1876, followed by Richard (7th February 1877), Franz (13th March 1878), Lina (25th February 1879), Eva (1st March 1883), Hugo (26th January 1884), Otto (19th February 1885), Maria (25th February 1887), and finally Ernst, born on 24th March 1890.

Friedrich and Anna Steiff's children were much loved by Margarete Steiff, as she herself could not have children due to her disability. And these children were to play not only a large role in Margarete's life, but above all they influenced and determined the history of Margarete Steiff GmbH decisively. While Margarete's brother ran a construction business, his children learned professions that qualified them to work in their aunt's toy factory.

Fig. 57: Margaret Steiff's motto, "For children, only the best is good enough," was first used in the 1892 catalogue.

THE COMPANY PROSPERS

Until this point, Margarete Steiff's company had developed in a rather contemplative and measured way, but that was soon to change. In comparison to the previous years, events fairly tumbled over each other. Karl Vallendor wrote:

> *During the following years, cutting, stuffing, the frame – in short all the parts – were brought to a more perfect level, and the spirit of Margarete Steiff presided over everything, never tiring, always personally giving instructions to the ever more numerous employees and watching over the realisation of her ideas. She was not bogged down by any economic theories; she let herself be led by her natural knowledge of human nature, and she acted according to it. With an iron will, good talent for observation and integrity toward her employees, Margarete Steiff followed her work, convinced by it, giving children unbreakable toys that were true playmates.*

It's possible that the famous quotation from Goethe, "...in art, the best is good enough", inspired the motto Margarete Steiff used for the first time in the 1892 catalogue: "For children, only the best is good enough!". This motto stood as a heading and the text that followed continued in the same vein:

> *Starting from this principle, we tried to make a toy that corresponded to all the right elements, both in durability as well as in the shape. In our play animals we use the best felt materials, made just for this purpose (also using plush and furs where the similarity to nature demands it), fine, soft stuffing material, and – to secure the shape – a springy metal frame.*
> *The wheels and other trimmings are mostly made according to our own designs and calculated to be as indestructible as possible.*
> *From very modest beginnings, our production rate has increased to 1,000 and more pieces per week meaning every contract can be fulfilled promptly.*
> *With the co-operation of artistic and technical personnel and the support of brilliant products from the leading, local felt factories at our disposal, we are able continually to perfect our toys whilst still increasing their numbers.*

Fig. 58: Outside back cover of the
1892 catalogue.

Fig. 59: Colour cover of the catalogue
'Felt toy factory' from 1892.

Fig. 60: The first part of the catalogue from 1892 comprises the toys.

Fig. 61: The second part of the catalogue from 1892 features the felt mail-order business.

At this point 256 toy products were available on 32 catalogue pages. Department I was dedicated to the "felt toy fabrication" and comprised 22 pages, while Department II, "mail-order felt", had ten pages.

The range of toys offered had multiplied in only two years. For the first time bears were in the range, though they still stood on four legs and were not movable. For the most part, the various types of animals were illustrated with small pictures.

Fig. 62–73 this page below and right:
Toy products offered in the catalogue of 1892.

Affen.

No. 48.

Kegelspiele.

No. 70. 55

Velocipedfahrende Tiere.

No. 80.

Katzen.

No. 95.

Pudelhunde.

Jagdhunde.

No. 30.

No. 40.

Giraffen.

No. 45.

Schafe.

No. 122.

Pferde mit Wagen.

No. 14.

THE FIRST TRADEMARK

Of course, news of the success that Margarete Steiff had with the production of soft stuffed toys got around very quickly. All of a sudden, there were a number of new producers who all wanted to profit from the promising new market. For Margarete Steiff this meant that she had to ask herself very early on how she could mark her high-quality products clearly and easily for the customer, so setting herself apart at first glance from the competition, which was mainly of lower quality. Another interesting innovation from the 1892 catalogue is worth mentioning in relation to this: the top right-hand corner of the cover showed a camel bearing the captions 'trademark'

Kameele.

No. 2.

No. 113.

Weichgestoppte kleine Scherztiere

an Gummischnur.

Thiere als Nadelkissen und Tintenwischer.

No. 138.

and 'protection of patterns and designs'. Unfortunately, apart from this appearance in the 1892 catalogue, there is no further information on whether it was used in any other capacity. We can assume, however, that it was a simple tag made of paper that was easy to remove and therefore not especially efficient. This assumption is based on the fact that the next two attempts of a label were also paper tags. A few examples of both of these different trademarks in paper have survived through the years. These are both stamped with an elephant with a raised trunk in the form of an S with the inscription 'M. St. Fabrikmarke' ('M. St. Factory Tag'). The later of the two also carries the additional words 'Gesetzl. geschützt – unzerbrechlich' or 'protected by law – unbreakable' (see also the illustrations above and the appendix, page 185). In the 1898 catalogue the demand for a trademark emphasising quality is underlined by the following remark:

> *I ask you to observe my factory brand, 'M. St. Elefant', and warn you of highly inferior quality imitations that have been seen recently. First felt toy factory in Germany.*

Another interesting reference can be found in the 1930 anniversary publication:

> *The first trademark was not the 'Button in Ear', but a picture of the first historic product – the elephant – with its trunk forming the S in 'M. St.'.*

THE NEW GENERATION STEPS UP

Clearly at this time toy production is the more important part of the business, but mail-order felt still plays a part. On 3rd March 1893, registration of the 'Filz-Spielwaren-Fabrik' (felt toy factory) in the registry of companies is finally completed. In 1877, a total of 3,065 marks worth of felt was bought from the Vereinigte Filzfabriken; in 1886 the total was 1,460 marks, in 1888 it was 3,700 marks, and in 1890 it was 5,070 marks. At the time of the company's registration in 1893 it had increased to 12,000 marks. By way of comparison, the average yearly income of a

Fig. 74 left: The camel is cited as the first trademark in the catalogue of 1892.

Fig. 75 centre: A few examples of the tag with the stamped elephant still exist.

Fig. 76 right: The elephant as the trademark – a first attempt to distance the company from the competition and protect against copying.

Fig. 77: The sewing department of the toy factory looked something like this (recreated photo).

teacher at this time was about 750 marks. The following year, in 1894, the felt toy factory hired a travelling salesman for the first time, a Mr P Morschheuser, equipping him with sample wares in felt. He was to extend the sales region. There is a passage on this topic in the 1930 anniversary publication:

> *The toy factory's business had so progressed by this point that registration in the registry of companies followed on 3rd March 1893 ... In this year the company had bought felt for 12,000 marks, a sum that also included felt for the felt mail-order business and felt clothing, which was still being manufactured. In 1894 a travelling salesman, Mr P Morschheuser, was given samples, which got our foot in the door of big cities.*

In August of the same year Margarete's father, Friedrich Steiff, died. Until the end he participated enthusiastically in the development and business success of his daughter, Margarete. He was able to see for himself how a great mainstay of the family had emerged from the child everyone used to worry about.

Margarete was now 47 years old. She had achieved what no one would have thought possible – despite being severely disabled she had not only become the founder and director of a successful company, she had also taken on the responsibility for her entire family.

Fig. 78: Margarete Steiff – successful entrepreneur and pillar of the family.

In 1897, ten employees were working in-house and there were a further 30 home-workers; the annual turnover was already 90,000 marks. It was at this point that Richard Steiff became the first of her nephews to begin his career in his aunt's company. Like his siblings, he had spent a great deal of time in his aunt's sewing workshop during his early childhood. After completing his business training at the Vereinigte Filzfabriken in Giengen and then attending a school for arts and crafts in Stuttgart, he was well prepared for his new tasks. In the same year, together with Mr Eulenstein from Baden-Baden (who later became the company's travelling salesman in Britain), he represented the company at the Leipzig Fair, where – for the first time – the company took its own stand. The anniversary publication reports:

> In 1897 Margarete Steiff's company, represented by Mr Richard Steiff, was an exhibitor for the first time at the Leipzig Fair, where there a great deal of contact was made with foreign companies. Since this time the company has exhibited uninterruptedly at the fair in Leipzig. Steiff toys have been sold at the fair since 1893, firstly through a fair representative at a stand in the Nikolai Church. The company itself exhibited for the first time in 1897 at a pub at Hainstraße 2, then in 1899 at Neumarkt 8, and since 1908 at the 'Meßpalast Monopol', which was joined with the 'Zentralmeßpalast' after its renovation in 1925.

Of course, the retail trade had long been aware of the company from Giengen and had ambitiously attempted to partake in the turnover of these innovative products. The wholesaler owned by Paul Wetzel, Söhlke Nachf. in Berlin, had considered

Fig. 79: Richard Steiff – the first of the nephews to enter his Aunt Margarete's company in 1897.

Fig. 80: The Steiff balcony showpiece at the
Leipzig Fair in 1930. Since 1897 Margarete
Steiff's company has exhibited there.

itself the only sales outlet for Steiff toys for Berlin and foreign markets since 1895.
In 1897, however, this distribution was given to the company G. F. Hertzog in
Berlin. At the same time, Mr Eulenstein began his job as a travelling salesman in
Britain.

In the next year, 1898, a second nephew began to work at the company. He was
the oldest son of Margarete's brother. Paul Steiff completed an apprenticeship
with the woodcarver and draughtsman Rupp, after which he worked for many
years at the church organ factory Gebr. Link; both of these businesses were located in Giengen. After that, he attended the school for arts and crafts in Stuttgart for
five terms. In between he was always engaged by his father for help in the construction company. Paul Steiff wrote the following regarding that:

> *Regardless of whether the father wouldn't wish upon his worst enemy working in a con-
> struction company in Giengen, he repeatedly forced his son Paul to do so for three
> months at a time. But business was so slow in the autumn that the father was forced
> to offer him to Marg. Steiff Filzversand & Spielwaren for that season and they soon
> asked him to join the company doing enlargements and reductions of patterns as well
> as designing and drawing them, and overseeing their application.*

Fig. 81 far left: Paul Steiff began his career in Aunt Margarete's company in 1898.

Fig. 82 left: Franz Steiff, like his brother Paul, began to work for Aunt Margarete in 1898.

Also in 1898, Franz Steiff became the third of Margarete Steiff's nephews to join the successful and continually aspiring business. His training background also brought valuable skills to the company. At the weaving school in Heidenheim and in the weaving mill of his uncle Albert Böckh in Aalen he completed his studies of weaving. Of course, all of this qualified him brilliantly to manufacture stuffed animals. The 1930 anniversary publication reported as follows:

> *Mr Franz Steiff dedicated his early years to the study of weaving and subsequently entered the business of his Aunt Margarete with this very valuable knowledge for the fabrication of stuffed animals in 1898. He mainly dedicated himself to the internal organisation of the company, the sale of materials, bookkeeping, and especially extending sales.*

All of the key positions were thus filled with family members. The expansion of the company continued with giant steps, not least because of these well-educated and highly motivated new employees. In 1899 Richard Steiff went on a trip to England with Mr Rabus of the Vereinigte Filzfabriken. In the same year the distribution of Steiff toys was awarded to Mr Herbert Hughes from London. Another distribution contract in Germany was awarded to Mr Hess in Hamburg.

Because of all this activity and expansion, space in the Giengen factory was soon once again too small. New rooms needed to be created, and quickly. The space between the two buildings built during the time from 1888 to 1890 was filled in with a new building in 1899. This new building housed the packing department of the toy factory.

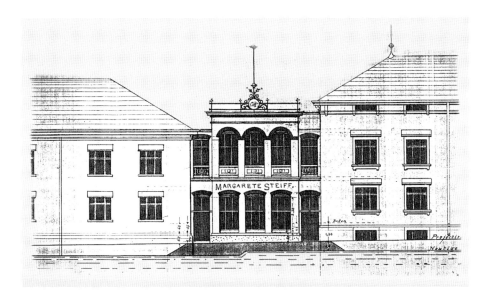

Fig. 83: In 1899, the gap between the buildings on Turmstraße is filled in by a new building housing the packing division of Margarete Steiff's toy factory.

Fig. 84 right: A sketch of the city of Giengen from the south west. The so-called Pulverturm that was bought by Friedrich Steiff in 1887 can still be seen here.

Fig. 85 far right: This sketch shows the same perspective after the demolition of the Pulverturm and with a view of the two planned buildings.

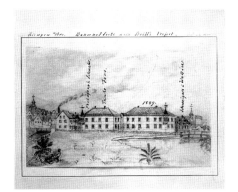

Fig. 86: A view of the buildings on Mühlstraße after completion of all three parts.

The first protection
of patterns and designs

In 1899 the first protection for the pattern and design of various toy animals was applied for at the county court in charge in Heidenheim. Thus each of the models was protected by the company – another step toward protection against the quite numerous competitor companies who were often bringing cheap copies of high-quality Steiff products into the marketplace.

Fig. 87: Excerpt from the registry of patterns and designs from 3rd June 1899. A copy in block writing can be found in the appendix (page 178).

Abb. 88: Velvet deer – article number 207 m (position 1 on the sample protection registration from 3rd June 1899).

Abb. 89: Velvet elephant – article number 424 m (position 2 on the sample protection registration from 3rd June 1899).

Abb. 90: Velvet fox terrier with brown and black spots – article number 468-4m (position 5 on the sample protection registration from 3rd June 1899).

Abb. 92: Monkey as coach-man – article number 591 g (position 16 on the sample protection registration from 3rd June 1899).

Abb. 94: Velvet dachshund – article number 461-2m (position 26 on the sample protection registration from 3rd June 1899).

Abb. 91: Dancing bear (bristle bear) – article number 581-5 (position 13 on the sample protection registration from 3rd June 1899).

Abb. 93: Bird hanging toy – article number 643-1 (position 22 on the sample protection registration from 3rd June 1899).

The numbers given in the registry excerpt (see Figure 87, above left) stand for the following animals (the article numbers that were valid at the time are in parentheses):

Pos. 01: 207 (207 m)	Velvet deer	
Pos. 02: 424 (424 m)	Velvet elephant	
Pos. 03: 459 (459-4)	Felt fox terrier with brown and black spots (17 cm)	
Pos. 04: 462 (462-4)	Felt fox terrier with brown and black spots (12 cm)	
Pos. 05: 468 (468-4m)	Velvet fox terrier with brown and black spots	
Pos. 06: 533 (533 m)	Lying velvet hare (12 cm)	
Pos. 07: 535 (535 m)	Lying velvet hare (10 cm)	
Pos. 08: 536 (536 m)	Lying velvet hare (8 cm)	
Pos. 09: 549 (549 m)	Begging velvet hare (22 cm)	
Pos. 10: 550 (550 m)	Begging velvet hare (14 cm)	
Pos. 11: 548 (548 m)	Velvet hare head	
Pos. 12: 555 (555-1)	Cycle-elephant	
Pos. 13: 581 (581-5)	Dancing bear	

Pos. 14: 591e (591 e)	Monkey as hussar
Pos. 15: 591f (591 f)	Monkey as infantryman
Pos. 16: 591g (591 g)	Monkey as coachman
Pos. 17: 591i (591 i)	Monkey as Cuban
Pos. 18: 605 (605-2m)	Lying velvet cat, painted (12 cm)
Pos. 19: 606.2m (606-2m)	Lying velvet cat, painted (10 cm)
Pos. 20: 606.m (606 m)	Sitting velvet cat, painted
Pos. 21: 601.m (601 m)	Standing velvet cat, painted
Pos. 22: 643 (643-1)	Bird hanging toy
Pos. 23: 715 (715-1)	Nansen with polar bear
Pos. 24: 716 (716-1)	Bear trainer with brown bear
Pos. 25: 1241, 42 & 43 (1241, 1242 & 1243)	Frog (12, 8 & 5 cm)
Pos. 26: 461 (461-2m)	Velvet dachshund

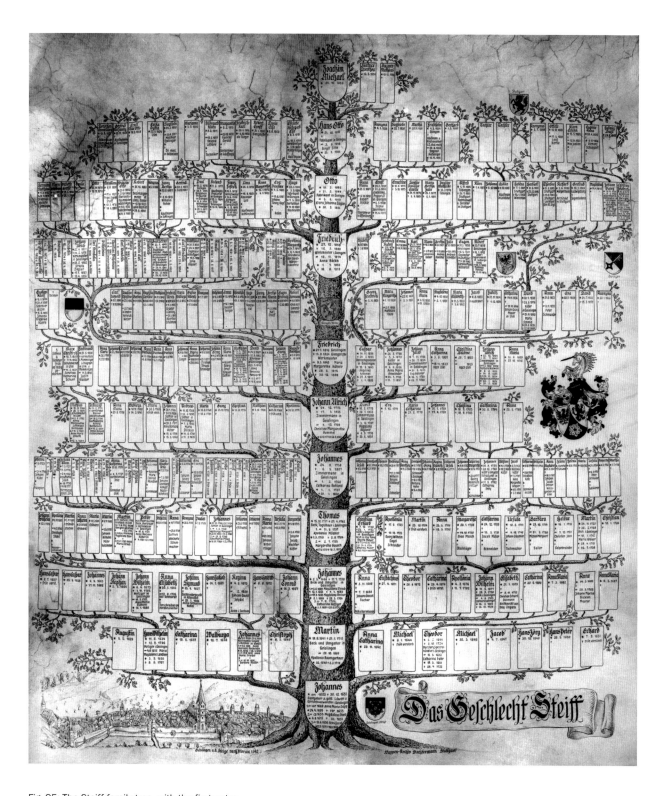

Fig. 95: The Steiff family tree, with the first entry
'around 1545', the last on 20th June 1914.

Fig. 96: The six sons of Friedrich Steiff in the order of their ages (from bottom to top: Paul, Richard, Franz, Hugo, Otto and Ernst) – a rather unconventional perspective.

THE NEW GENERATION IS CHALLENGED

Margarete's brother Friedrich Steiff died on 16th March 1900. He was only 52 years old. His death came not entirely unexpectedly, however, for he had not been in the best of health for some time. Nevertheless, this was an occasion of deep grief for the whole family. His son Paul Steiff characterised his father with the following words:

> *In their family* [AUTHOR'S NOTE: THE FAMILY OF FRIEDRICH AND ANNA STEIFF] *a true Christian spirit and good discipline were the order of the day. From early on, the sons were raised to take part in their father's construction company and they were expected to follow similar careers: their father did not want to raise any civil servants since he did not believe them to be independent people. So, the sons all enjoyed good educations and their health developed pleasingly. ... In the last years of his life, when his health was already failing, Friedrich Steiff – using clever construction policies – made it possible for Margarete Steiff's company to purchase cheap land, which brought her a great advantage. He also spent a great deal of time and energy in putting up a central building for providing the city with electric light and power.*

Friedrich Steiff not only recognised very early the business opportunities which manufacturing of felt toys would create for his sister Margarete. Looking to the future, he also planned for the company's expansion and the space that would be needed for it. It was not only his family who had much to thank his intelligence and level-headedness for, as well as his talent, but also Margarete Steiff's company. Of course, Margarete Steiff knew that too. Community feeling had been very characteristic of the family up to that point, but at this time they pulled even closer together. Three of her brother's nine children – Paul, Richard and Franz – already held responsible positions in their aunt's business.

The oldest daughter, Lina Steiff, was also employed by the company as the director of the sewing department from 1898 until her wedding to Alexander Leo, a Munich industrialist, on 18th September 1905. Her sister Eva was responsible for

Fig. 97: Leonhard Meck was hired by Margarete Steiff in 1900. He was in charge of sales and from 1907 was given general commercial power of attorney at Margarete Steiff GmbH.

managing the branches, with the task of receiving and assigning work from the homeworkers. Since at that time this included a branch in Aalen, she met her future husband, businessman Georg Köpff, the son of ox dealer Wilhelm Köpff from Göppingen, through her work with her aunt. His ancestors also originally came from Gussenstadt (see family tree on page 70) and are mentioned in a document with the Steiff ancestors, whose early roots also lie in Gussenstadt. The wedding took place on 15th July 1907.

There is no evidence that Friedrich Steiff's youngest daughter, Maria, ever worked regularly in the toy factory. She married the teacher Robert Blickle on 5th October 1910.

Margarete's widowed sister Pauline Röck had also been employed by the company since 1892 and, two years previously, in 1890 Emilie Häußler, the oldest daughter of Margarete's sister Marie, who had died prematurely, had also found employment with her aunt.

Thus, there remain three of Friedrich's sons to account for: Hugo, Otto and Ernst. They also soon found positions in their aunt's company. Margarete Steiff never forgot the decision she had made when her sister Marie had died so early in 1879 – that she would care for her siblings and their offspring for their entire lives – and she put that decision into effect in an incomparable manner.

But it was not just members of the family who were given top positions in the company. What counted first and foremost were qualification and performance, for the company was growing unstoppably. And thus additional suitable and well-educated employees were needed. In 1900 Leonhard Meck was hired by Margarete Steiff to take over the direction of what had become the extensive sales department. In 1907 he was granted general commercial power of attorney. This is what the 1930 anniversary publication has to say of him:

> *The company secretary, Mr Meck, was of great service in seeing that the company bloomed and many of our customers recall the pleasant time they had working with him. An illness that he paid too little attention to, due to his ambitious professional life, tore him from the loving atmosphere of his sphere of activity in 1926.*

Fig. 98: Margarete Steiff, surrounded by employees in front of the finished buildings on Mühlstraße.

In 1900 the company had 30 employees and another 54 women were working as homeworkers. The annual turnover was 188,000 marks. Another foreign distribution outlet, this time in Italy, was added. It was awarded to G. Pansier's company in Florence. After England and Italy, in 1901 the third foreign representative was added, H. Kamp in Amsterdam, Holland. In this year the last separate catalogue was published for the felt mail-order business. It opens with the following words:

Alongside my felt toy-making business I have managed a felt mail-order business for years with great success. I feel honoured to send you the following samples to look through, for which net prices are marked.

The felt mail-order business had finally become a triviality. The catalogue had only seven pages. And on the last page little toy animals made of velvet were already being offered under the heading "Knick-knacks and pin cushions".

Meanwhile, unlike the clothing business, almost every year a new catalogue was published featuring felt toys. "For children, only the best is good enough! Always

73

Fig. 99: Cover of the last catalogue for the felt mail-order business of 1901.

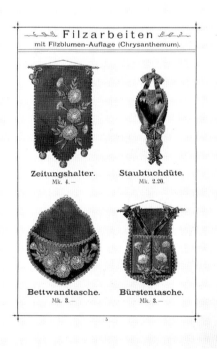

Fig. 100: Felt articles of varying types (page 5 of the catalogue for the felt mail-order business from 1901).

Fig. 101: An article from Margarete Steiff's mail-order business – a pillow cover made of felt.

Fig. 102: Cover of the felt toy catalogue from 1901.

loyal to this principle I am now sending my sixth illustrated price list out into the world." This is the introduction from the toy catalogue of 1901. The motto of the first catalogue from 1892 hadn't changed – and it won't change, for it has remained valid to the present day. The illustrated price list of 1901 comprising 38 pages, was written in German, English, and French, and contained almost 500 different animals. Margarete Steiff's energy seems boundless. She carried the entire responsibility for her company and was always in the know about every single detail. In Steiff's archives there remains a wealth of letters and copies of letters written in her own hand, mainly correspondence with suppliers and customers, but there are also many notes to her nieces and nephews. She was available for her employees and, naturally, for her family at all times. She was a prudent, responsible and conscientious entrepreneur and an attentive and helpful woman who always cared about the good of her fellow human beings.

The three oldest nephews, Richard, Paul and Franz, began to take on more and more responsibility, and had matured into pillars of the company. Although

Fig. 103: Margarete Steiff
at her desk.

Richard occupied himself more with the business management of the company at first, his inventiveness qualified him more and more for the area of toy development and manufacture. In the anniversary publication of 1930 Karl Vallendor wrote the following about him:

Fig. 104 below left: So that she could reach
the workshops in her wheelchair, Margarete
Steiff had a ramp added to the buildings on
Turmstraße.

Fig. 105 below: Margarete Steiff on her way
to her offices.

> *... he dedicated himself fully to the design and manufacture of soft stuffed toys and con-*
> *tributed many new ideas. The company has to thank his initiative for generating new*
> *ideas within the company and also for bringing in new approaches from outside the*
> *organisation.*

Fig. 106: Margarete Steiff
with her niece Eva and
Eva's daughter Margarete.

Fig. 107: Children of homeworkers
transport wares up the ramp on
Turmstraße.

Paul Steiff continued to be in charge of creating patterns and making models of new products. Additionally, he occupied himself continually with the development of the various voices that have been installed inside the toy animals since the early years.

Franz Steiff's areas of responsibility also became more extensive. Alongside the organisation of the company, purchasing, and bookkeeping, he was in charge of building up representation and of establishing sample warehouses in Berlin, Hamburg, Milan, London and Amsterdam.

In general, foreign markets were becoming more and more important for the toy factory. Already in 1898 Margarete Steiff had recognised the importance of foreign markets and pointed out the "growing export turnover" in her catalogue of the same year. Only at the beginning of the twentieth century do the efforts around these markets bring extraordinary results. Paul Steiff went to the US for almost two years. Franz Steiff took care of Britain where – taking the time spent on all of his trips together – he also passed the equivalent of many years.

Fig. 108 left: An advertising postcard that Paul Steiff handed out
during his trip to the US.

Fig. 109 above: The postcard that Richard
Steiff sent from Paris to his brother Paul
in New York in July 1902.

And, on the continent, Richard Steiff visited Germany's neighbouring countries.
Richard wrote the following from Paris to his brother Paul in New York in 1902:

> I sold just Spitze [AUTHOR'S NOTE: PLUSH POMERANIANS] to Bon Marché here for 7-
> 8,000 francs. The French are beginning to take note. Turnover will double, compared with
> last year, for France. I have my notebook filled with new things. Dieckmann hardly has
> any samples here and began with the simplest things (pin cushions) as you know. In the
> large emporiums I have seen our things in different departments. ... Velvet animals are
> being made everywhere now, but only rubbish, I am not afraid of competition. ... A branch
> in France would not be worth it, customs and freight are only 10-15 per cent.
>
> Best, Richard

On 2nd September 1902 he wrote to New York again, but this time from Moscow:

> Today, on the third day, Moscow is already no more foreign to me than Berlin. Every
> third Russian seems to understand German. I have completely fulfilled the goal of this
> trip, to sound out Russia.   Best, Richard

How close the siblings were not only professionally but also personally becomes
clear from some other lines from Richard's letter:

> The style of the 500 churches here would really make you fume – they are gold-plated
> inside and out. I only need to get a whiff of the inside; it stinks. I've been here for four
> days and see no more point to it. The overwhelming view of a sunset on this colourful-

78

Fig. 111: Otto Steiff began his career with a business apprenticeship in his Aunt Margarete's company in 1902.

Fig. 110: On 2nd September 1902, Richard Steiff wrote a postcard from Moscow to his brother Paul in New York.

ly shimmering city has left me as full as after a Russian dinner. Shorovsky has shown me the finest and most interesting places. One day we were out on the tiles until 7 in the morning and guzzled 200 marks (which he paid) just on food and drinks.

Hundreds of letters and postcards from this time are kept in the Steiff archives. Most of them have been left by Paul Steiff, who meticulously put all of the documents in order and very often marked them with his comments. The correspondence available proves how promptly those in charge at the toy factory informed others of the current opportunities and events, regardless of where they happened to be in the world at the time. This correspondence bears witness to why Margarete Steiff's company was already so extraordinarily successful at this time.

Otto Steiff, second youngest son of Margarete's brother Friedrich Steiff, began his three-year apprenticeship as a businessman at the Steiff company in 1902 after attending a secondary school in Heidenheim. After successfully completing this education, he graduated from the school of commerce in Cologne in 1905. After that, he worked as one of the toy factory's business directors. The 1930 anniversary publication has this to say about him:

> Mr Otto Steiff has dedicated his energy to the company for the past 28 years. He decided upon business management. After ending his studies at the school of commerce in Cologne, he joined the business where he has been a managing director since 1909.

Fig. 112: The first images of 'Bear 55 PB' from the catalogue of new products 1903/1904, the prototype of today's Teddy bear.

'BEAR 55 PB'

Two further events that would have decisive consequences on the future development of Margarete Steiff's company also took place in the year 1902. Richard Steiff was responsible for both. One was the planning and preparation for the toy factory's avant-garde new building, for which construction was to commence the following year. Even more important, however, was the invention of a small, movable toy animal made of plush that received the product code 'Bear 55 PB'. Richard Steiff developed the first jointed bear, the prototype of today's Teddy bear. For more background and details of circumstances accompanying the invention of the Teddy bear, as well as its development, please refer to the book 100 Years Steiff Teddy Bears that was published in 2002 on the occasion of the toy's 100th anniversary. You will find an abridged version of the creation of the Teddy bear in the appendix (page 180). What this new development meant for the company is succinctly summarised by Karl Vallendor in the 1930 anniversary publication:

Fig. 113 above: Theodore 'Teddy' Roosevelt lent his name to the Teddy bear.

> *The American President Theodore Roosevelt, a passionate bear hunter, had just come to office. When the first examples of the new bear came to the US, the Americans took the funny little chap for a national symbol of the 'happy huntings' of their president and called him 'Teddy' bear. Everyone had to have a 'Teddy', and already in the first year 12,000 examples of this still popular toy animal sailed across the ocean. Thus, 'Teddy' became famous all over the world overnight, as well as becoming a milestone in Steiff's further development.*

Fig. 114 right: Richard Steiff with his invention, the Teddy bear.

Fig. 115: The east building was built in 1903 according to Richard Steiff's drawings.

THE GLASS BUILDINGS –
A PIECE OF COURAGEOUS ARCHITECTURE

Of course, the great demand for Teddy bears required the expansion of both the production process and the production rooms. It was more by happy coincidence than foresight that plans for the new buildings had been underway since 1902, and on 28th January 1903 an application to build was submitted to the city. This was the only way in which the immense growth in volume could be coped with at all. The first glass building, the east building with an area of 1,080 m^2, was finished in 1903 after a construction period of a little more than six months. By 1904 the west building was also already completed. The newer glass building was much larger and comprised 6,840 m^2 of working area.

The east building was an iron-and-glass construction, a very unusual way of build-ing in this period. In the west building, erected in 1904, the weight-bearing parts were mostly made of wood rather than steel, although the principle of the glass

Fig. 116: Only one year later, in 1904, the much bigger west building followed.

Fig. 117: Richard Steiff and his wife Else, née Dehlinger.

façade was retained. The idea for these cost-effective 'glass houses', so excellently suited to making toys, came from Richard Steiff. Margarete Steiff gave him a free hand, for he had discussed all of the plans extensively with her and his brothers. However, she insisted expressly on the addition of a ramp which made it possible for her to enter the building. Today, Margarete Steiff GmbH's headquarters is still based in these buildings (the ramp has naturally since been removed); since 1980, they are protected by being listed as 'historical monuments'. In Chapter 7 (page 152), further details of these extraordinary buildings are described.

Also in his personal life Richard Steiff had much to be happy about in 1904. On 25th May he married Else Emma Dehlinger (born 10th October 1882), who was the daughter of Theodor Dehlinger and his wife Elise, née Müller.

Fig. 118: The ramp built especially for Margarete Steiff can be clearly seen on this photograph.

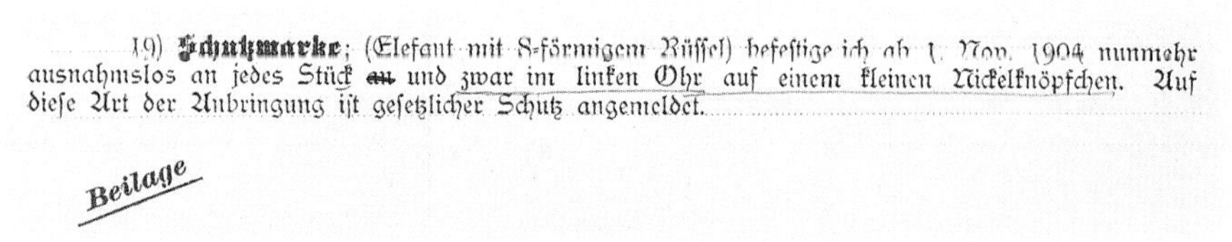

19) **Schutzmarke**: (Elefant mit S-förmigem Rüssel) befestige ich ab 1. Nov. 1904 nunmehr ausnahmslos an jedes Stück an und zwar im linken Ohr auf einem kleinen Nickelknöpfchen. Auf diese Art der Anbringung ist gesetzlicher Schutz angemeldet.

Beilage

Fig. 119: An excerpt from the publication of 1904 that announced that the 'Button in Ear' would from then on be the trademark.

Fig. 120: Front and back of the medal won at the World's Fair in 1904.

'BUTTON IN EAR'

In 1904 the company was finally successful in developing a practical and, above all, lasting solution to the problem of labelling Steiff toys. Franz Steiff can be called the inventor of the trademark 'Button in Ear'. The 1930 anniversary publication dedicated only one short sentence linking this brilliant business idea to Franz Steiff: "The trademark 'Button in Ear' was also his idea." If nothing else, this sentence delivers us proof today of the authorship of this unmistakable Steiff company trademark. Elsewhere, the anniversary publication is very clear about the significance of the trademark:

> *It was a comforting thought to rivet a Steiff button in the ear of every animal and a targeted and continuing marketing campaign hammered the idea into a large portion of our audience, fixing the notion of first-class, quality wares.*

Margarete Steiff marketed the new development immediately. Under point 19 of an information flyer that began with the words, "Forthwith I politely ask you to take note of the following," the following fact was announced:

> *Trademark: (elephant with S-shaped trunk) beginning on 1st November 1904, I will attach a small nickel button to the left ear of invariably every piece. Legal protection is registered for this type of fastening.*

Fig. 121: The Grand Prize certificate won in St Louis in 1904.

With the so-called 'elephant' button, an unique marking for Steiff animals was finally achieved, thus separating them from the ever more numerous copies and cheap products of the competition. It represented only the beginning of the Steiff identification markings that are attached to every Steiff animal, even today. A detailed description of all Steiff markings can be found in the appendix (page 185).

Fig. 122: Work was done at long
tables in the new glass buildings.

THE CHANGE IN GENERATIONS ARRIVES —
THE FOUNDING OF THE LIMITED COMPANY (GMBH)

The new company buildings prove to be an excellent investment. In the light and airy rooms of the glass buildings the production moves forward well. In 1904, 12,000 of the new bears alone were manufactured. And the work is worth it: Franz Steiff exhibited at the World's Fair in St. Louis in 1904. There the company won the grand prize and Margarete and Richard Steiff each won a gold medal.

The organisation of the production processes was refined more and more and perfected. Thus, a new product code system was introduced in 1905 – the item or article number. Each article received a four-digit number. Each of the individual numbers allowed one to see directly the animal's material, composition and size, as well as any special finishing. This system made working in many areas quite a bit easier and was only replaced by a more modern system in 1968. The details of the article numbering system are explained in the appendix (page 176).

And the next wedding was announced in 1905. Paul Steiff married Wilhelmine Schneider, daughter of Wilhelm August and Susanne Schneider (née Maier), on 18th September.

Hugo Steiff completed his education in 1906 and began immediately thereafter to work in his aunt's company, putting his new knowledge into practice. An apprenticeship in the agricultural machine factory, Joh. Eckhardt and Son, and an ensuing job in the machine factory of his uncle Matthäus Steiff in Schorndorf allowed him to amass a good knowledge of mechanical engineering. After two years at the engineering school in Mannheim and military service in the German Grenadier Guards regiment in Karlsruhe, as well as successfully completing his exams, his tasks now lay in the technical area of the company. With the enlarging of the factory grounds and the further extension of the machine equipment in the individual departments, he found a great deal of room in which to be active.

Although Margarete Steiff was now actively supported by five of her six nephews, her own enthusiasm for the company remained undiminished. She was now 58 years old and not a bit tired, even if, as we know from her eulogy (see appendix, page 182), she did suffer from insomnia. She acted cleverly and in a forward-looking manner. Because of her great level-headedness, she did not forget to think about the future during these years of her toy factory's seemingly unstoppable upward motion. At the company, it was her three nephews, who had been in the company now for nearly ten years, who carried almost more responsibility than she herself. The expertise, competence, talent and productivity of Richard, Paul and Franz made for a great deal of the great company's success.

This was documented for the outside world and above all legally on 30th May 1906 when Margarete Steiff GmbH was established (the equivalent of creating a limited company). The capital investment when the GmbH was registered comprised 420,000 marks, of which Margarete Steiff took over 270,000, Richard 88,000, Paul 32,000, and Franz Steiff 30,000. At the same time nephews Richard, Paul and Franz were made managing directors alongside Margarete Steiff.

Ernst Steiff, the youngest nephew of Margarete, did not yet belong to the circle of those who were in a position to take over a responsible position within the company. He first attended a boys' school in Wilhelmsdorf, after which he completed an apprenticeship as a mechanic in his aunt's company. Since that did still not complete his education, he studied at the technical college for precision engineering in Schwenningen. Because of the outbreak of World War I and a trip to the US, he only returned to the family company in 1927.

Fig. 123: Hugo Steiff – after successfully completing engineering school he began his career at the toy factory in 1906.

Fig. 124: Ernst Steiff first completed an apprenticeship as a mechanic at Margarete Steiff GmbH. But it was only in 1927 that he returned to the company.

EXCITING TIMES

With expansion into other European lands, Steiff GmbH's growth continued in its year of foundation: in 1906 Töpfer in Leipzig was awarded the distribution contract for both the Scandinavian countries Norway and Sweden.

In the same year a phenomenal 385,393 Teddy bears were sold. The following year – which went down as the 'bear year' in the history of the company – this number increased even more, reaching an unprecedented 973,999 pieces. The lion's share of these Teddy bears went to the American market, but even in Germany and other European countries the demand for these neat new playmates increased greatly. The entire annual production, meaning all of the play products manufactured in 1907, comprised 1,700,000 pieces. Achieving such numbers required 400 employees at the factory and another 1,800 working as homeworkers or in branches. This was an exceptional organisational achievement, hiring so many new employees in such a short time, training them, and integrating them into the existing production

Fig. 125: Margarete Steiff with head of purchasing, Edmund Steiner, of the American wholesaler Hilder & Brothers in New York.

processes or, where necessary, even developing new concepts – not to forget that people's mobility back then was quite restricted. Franz Steiff was responsible for building up and co-ordinating the outside branches. Karl Vallendor wrote in the anniversary publication:

> *Mr Franz Steiff was also the organiser in charge of the eight fabrication and delivery branches for homeworking in neighbouring cities and areas during the years 1906-1908; these were necessary as the company could otherwise no longer meet the demand for goods.*

The company's production figures were not the only occasion for joy. There were a lot of personal reasons to celebrate as well: on 15th June 1907 two marriages were celebrated in the Steiff household. Franz Steiff married Klara Steiff, the daughter of the official building contractor of Geislingen, Georg Ernst Steiff. And his sister Eva had her own wedding ceremony at the same time.

There was also bad news in this year. In the US, the economic crisis broke out. Large contracts were cancelled. On the other hand, the company had to accept and pay for extensive plush orders that were made due to the expected continous high turnover. This was an exceptionally difficult and dangerous situation that hit the company at a sensitive time, in the middle of a phase of great upturn. Vallendor wrote the following:

Fig. 126: Franz Steiff and his wife Klara.

> *As no business remained untouched by the setbacks, the 'bear factory', as it was called back then, was hit as well. American economics were severely shaken in 1907 by an economic crisis that had a great effect on the company in Giengen. The large orders for bears – most of them were already finished and ready for shipping in the warehouse – were cancelled, and large amounts of ordered plush also had to be accepted. The managers needed all their prudence and strength to overcome this setback.*

Now the many trips and massive advertising activities in almost all European countries paid off. The loss of contracts in the US couldn't be fully compensated for but, thanks to a growing number of orders from Germany and the rest of Europe, Steiff could avoid a serious crisis. Obvious confirmation of this state of affairs was the completion of the third glass building in 1908. The north building contained another 6,120 m^2 of workspace. Margarete Steiff GmbH now had at its disposal workspace totalling 14,040 m^2.

Fig. 127: Margarete Steiff GmbH's buildings in 1908.

Fig. 128: Lively bustle between the west and north buildings. The years of their erection (1904 and 1908) can be seen on the buildings.

Fig. 129: The 'Roloplan', a tailless, foldable kite
made of fabric, was also one of Richard Steiff's
inventions.

Again two foreign distribution contracts were awarded, going this time to Austria's
Schnötzinger in Vienna and Portugal's Rodrigues in Lisbon.
And in 1908 it was again Richard Steiff who pioneered a new invention. This time
it was a "tailless, foldable kite made of fabric" with the name of 'Roloplan'. Within just a short space of time this 'flying instrument' developed into a bestseller for
the company and remained so for many decades.

Giengen a. Br., den 10. Mai 1909.

Todes-Anzeige.

Am Sonntag den 9. Mai nachts 11¾ Uhr entschlief sanft, nach plötzlich aufgetretenem schwerem Leiden, im 62. Lebensjahr unsere innigst geliebte Schwester, Schwägerin, unser aller unvergeßliche Tante

Fräulein **Margarete Steiff,**
Gründerin der Spielwarenfabrik.

In tiefer Trauer:

Pauline Röck Witwe geb. **Steiff.**
Anna Steiff, Witwe des † **Fritz Steiff.**
Paul Steiff & Frau Mini geb. **Schneider.**
Richard Steiff & Frau Else geb. **Dehlinger.**
Klara Steiff, Witwe des † **Franz Steiff.**
Lina Leo geb. **Steiff & Alexander Leo.**
Eva Köpff geb. **Steiff & Georg Köpff.**
Hugo Steiff.
Otto Steiff.
Marie Steiff.
Ernst Steiff.
Susanna Jooss geb. **Hähnle,** Tante.
Michael Häussler, Schwager.
Emilie Wolff geb. **Häußler & Paul Wolff.**
Pauline Maier geb. **Häussler & Leonhard Maier.**

Die Beerdigung findet statt am Mittwoch den 12. Mai nachmittags ½2 Uhr.

Giengen-Brenz, den 10. Mai 1909.

Todes-Anzeige.

Nach kurzer Krankheit wurde gestern Nacht im 62. Lebensjahr

Fräulein **Margarete Steiff,**
die Gründerin der Spielwarenfabrik,

mitten aus ihrem Lebenswerk abberufen.

Die teure Entschlafene begann vor 30 Jahren unzerbrechliche Tierfiguren für ihren Freundschaftskreis eigenhändig anzufertigen. Ihre unermüdliche Schaffensfreude, Energie und vielseitige Begabung hat es ermöglicht, aus diesem kleinen Anfang das Geschäft zu der heutigen Bedeutung zu führen.

Wir werden das Geschäft in unveränderter Weise weiter führen und bitten um Ihr ferneres Wohlwollen.

Mit Hochachtung

Margarete Steiff G. m. b. H.

Paul Steiff.   Richard Steiff.

Fig. 130: An obituary announcement placed by the family upon Margarete Steiff's death.

Fig. 131: With this notification, Margarete Steiff GmbH announced the death of its founder on 10th May 1909.

THE OLD GENERATION STEPS DOWN

On 19th June 1908 Franz Steiff died at the age of only 30 years after a short, severe illness. Less than one year after she was married, Klara Steiff became a widow. Klara had to find a way of dealing with this incredibly difficult stroke of fate, and she did so by throwing herself into her work. Only a short time after the unexpected death of her husband, she began her energetic career at Margarete Steiff GmbH.

In Giengen the shock of Franz Steiff's death had not even sunk in when fate struck again: on 9th May 1909, a good two months before her 62nd birthday, Margarete Steiff died. Two weeks previously she had fallen ill with pneumonia. Despite that, her death came suddenly and unexpectedly.

The next day two obituary notices had already been published. The one sponsored by the company was signed by the two remaining managing directors, Paul and Richard Steiff, and stated that the family was grieving their "dearly beloved sister, sister-in-law, and our unforgettable aunt".

On 12th May 1909, Appolonia Margarete Steiff was buried in Giengen's cemetery. The eulogy was printed in a little flyer. Its complete content is reprinted here in the appendix (page 182).

Fig. 132: Margarete Steiff was accompanied by a seemingly endless funeral procession on the way to her final resting place.

Fig. 133: The coffin containing the mortal remains of Margarete Steiff was carried in a carriage loaded with wreaths and pulled by one white and one black horse.

Worte am Grabe

von

† Apollonia

Margarete Steiff

in

Giengen a. Br.

Geboren Giengen a. Br. 24. Juli 1847.
Gestorben „ „ „ 9. Mai 1909.
Beerdigt daselbst 12. Mai 1909.

Stpf. Siegle.

Fig. 134: Cover of the brochure containing Margarete Steiff's eulogy.

Fig. 135: Margarete Steiff's grave at Giengen's cemetery. Today it is still visited in remembrance by many people to show their respect.

Margarete Steiff's estate

Up to the day of her death, and despite being severely disabled, Margarete Steiff led a fulfilled life. She lived through the upswing of her toy factory and departed this life a successful, universally loved and respected entrepreneur. The size of the company founded and built by her put her in a position to give many people work, thus bringing an entire region prosperity. Because of her impressive entrepreneurial successes, but also because of her important services to the economy, Margarete Steiff is counted as one of the great female leaders of industry.

In private too she, a modest person dependent upon support in her daily life, helped her family to considerable fortune and alleviated the position of many people in need. As prudent as she was in her life, Margarete Steiff also took care of the time after her death. With the transformation of the company into its limited form in 1906, as well as in her clever and fair will and testament, she guaranteed the seamless continuation of her life's work. Her spirit lives on today in the company's beautiful products and in the motto that continues to flourish: "For children, only the best is good enough!"

Fig. 136: Margarete Steiff visiting the Giengen children's festival.

Fig. 137: Margarete Steiff's wheelchair is
pushed by her nephew Paul.

Fig. 138: Margarete
Steiff surrounded by
her family and closest
employees.

Fig. 139: Margarete Steiff
surrounded by employees.

In her last will and testament, Margarete Steiff made a specific legacy of 28,300 marks. So, in 1909, her sister Pauline received 20,000
marks, Margarete Rabus 3,000 marks, Lotte Maier 1,300 marks, and
her loyal lifetime companion Johanna Röck 1,000 marks. Another
3,000 marks were used to create a foundation. After subtracting this
legacy from the entire estate of 540,962.80 marks, the remaining
512,662.80 marks were divided evenly among her remaining nieces
and nephews. Thus the eight children of her brother Friedrich –
Paul, Richard, Hugo, Otto, Maria, Ernst, Lina (Leo) and Eva
(Köpff) – and the two children of her sister Marie – Emilie (Wolff)
and Pauline (Maier) – each received 51,266.28 marks.

During a meeting of the partners that took place after the will had
been read, an increase in the company's capital from 420,000 to
630,000 marks was decided upon. The division of the shares of the
business was then ordered as follows: Richard Steiff 192,000 marks,
Paul Steiff 108,000 marks, Hugo and Otto Steiff 60,000 marks each,
Lina Leo and Eva Köpff 54,000 marks each, and Maria and Ernst
Steiff 51,000 marks each.

Otto and Hugo Steiff were each made a managing director. Now four
nephews as managing directors and a total of eight nieces and
nephews as partners determined the future of Margarete Steiff
GmbH. The allocation of the company, still owned by the family
today, could be managed consensually and without damage to the
company – not at least thanks to Margarete's farseeing last will.

Opportunities and challenges

IV.

THE ERA AFTER MARGARETE STEIFF

Fig. 140: Following the death of Margarete Steiff the next generation took over responsibility for the company.

Fig. 141: Lina Leo, one of Margarete Steiff's nieces, became one of the company's partners after her aunt's death.

For almost 30 years Margarete Steiff was the person who made the decisions, and everything in the company she founded revolved around her – but above all, it was her personal presence which was always felt. Slowly but surely, people in Giengen got used to her death and the fact that they would have to do without her presence – so highly regarded – from then on. At the company, however, this type of sensitivity was not taken into consideration. Daily business had to go on in its usual way. Fortunately, there were no difficulties of an organisational kind. The company's destiny was in good hands, those of nephews Paul, Richard, Hugo and Otto, each of whom had held a position of managing director at Margarete Steiff GmbH.

FAMILY SQUABBLES

Admittedly, the house of Steiff was not always peaceful. From time to time there were family differences. What families are always in perfect agreement – especially when new people and new interests are constantly added to the game through marriage?

Lina Leo, for example, would have liked her husband Alexander, a businessman in Munich, to have taken on a leading position at Steiff in the days when Margarete was still alive. This problem, never quite resolved, became acute again after the company was reorganised. It seems it was mainly Richard and Paul who were not especially enthusiastic about the idea. But a discussion to clear things up never took place. Thus, a great deal of ill will developed among the siblings. As a result, Eva Köpff wrote a remarkable letter to her brothers Richard and Paul on 22nd December 1909:

> My dear brothers,
> When I think about the two letters I have received from Lina lately, I have to say firstly that the argument between her or, more precisely, between Alexander and her brothers must not continue any longer. Above all, we need to come to an agreement for the sake of her health, but of course we owe it to our dear Aunt Gretle as well. ... Because of Aunt Gretle's death, we are all more or less dependent upon each other to keep the business – so well managed by our brothers – up where it belongs, and only agreement among ourselves makes it strong. ... While following my thoughts as I lie in my bed, I feel more and more as a mother that it is our holy obligation to retain

Fig. 142: Eva Köpff, also one of Margarete Steiff's nieces. Almost one hundred years ago she wrote a letter to her brothers expressing her concerns for the company.

what our dear father and Aunt Gretle have left us, namely to keep the peace and to thank God for his favour and goodness. ...

With heartfelt regards,
Your sister, Eva

It is the following comment that is the most remarkable: "... to retain what our dear father and Aunt Gretle have left us". Remarkable because Friedhelm Steiff made the same statement almost word for word while giving the interview for this book, almost one hundred years after his Aunt Eva Köpff wrote this letter. This is an impressive illustration of how the company founder's attitude of mind has been permanently present even into the modern day.

Fig. 143: Hugo Steiff and his wife Hertha.

ADVERTISING – SHOWPIECES AND SCHLOPSNIES

Apart from the family squabbles described above, toward the end of the first decade of the new century there were no problems worth mentioning in the company. No one could complain about the turnover at the time. Compared with 1908, the number of pieces sold increased a good 15 per cent to almost one million toys. Measured against the record year 1907 this was still a comparatively low number, but it was heading upward. The following year, 1910, saw the positive trend continuing. The production increased anew, this time around eight per cent.

And finally, there was again occasion to celebrate in the family: Hugo Steiff got married. On 7th May 1910, Hertha Kögel became his wife. Born in October 1890, she was the daughter of Karl Viktor Kögel, the district notary, and his wife Elisabeth Kathrine (née Dürr).

The house of Steiff does not know the meaning of 'standing still'. In 1910, new construction plans were hatched. An annex was added

to the recently built north building in which a carpentry department was to be located. Since the glass buildings turned out to be so successful, the annex was also done in this style. Steiff now had at its disposal a production area of 15,120m2 under glass.

Even that did not represent the last innovation that year. Right from the beginning, the company was very aware of the importance of advertising, both for individual products and for establishing the company name. Therefore, the company placed a great deal of value on the design of advertising materials. At the Leipzig Fair of 1910 the company went down an entirely new path. 'Steiff Showpiece' was the magic phrase. This was a large decorative structure, put together from products from the existing range and custom-made accessories – and it caused a great sensation in Leipzig!

Sensational was also the way to describe the success that Steiff had with this type of advertising. The showpiece displayed in 1910 in Leipzig, called, 'Barrack Yard' had enthusiastic visitors standing in packed rows to see it. It was then an easy decision to continue advertising to large audiences in this way, publicising the company's own products and winning over new customers. These decorative pieces did not yet move, but that was soon to change.

In the autumn of the same year the Wertheim department store in Berlin showed the first mechanical showpiece, 'The Great Steiff Circus'. To make sure that the design and structure of this large display were perfect, Albert Schlopsnies was persuaded to work for the company on a freelance basis. The anniversary publication of 1930 reports details of this sensational performance:

In the autumn of 1910 Wertheim in Berlin presented 'The Great Steiff Circus', which was long the topic of conversation in Berlin. It had several rings and was designed by

Fig. 144: More than 15,000 m² of glass buildings make for an imposing scene.

Fig. 145: An excerpt from the mechanical showpiece 'Circus Sarrasani', which was shown publicly for the first time in Berlin in 1910.

Schlopsnies exactly in the style of the Circus Sarrasani. Many groups were mechanically driven and performed for the viewer a faithful re-enactment of the movements of circus acrobats. Here are some of the numbers performed in the humorous programme:

- Camels and dromedaries: riding high on the humps

- Six white Russian horses, trained in the wild but here stuffed and sewn up, with steel pipes for bones

- Ging-Geng-Gang, 'hair-raising' entertainers with their own long pigtails

- Twelve felt elephants from Württemburg of all ages, from swinging in the cradle to swinging in the park

- Japanese bamboo and toe artists – not only are they using wood and wool for their tricks they have wood and wool for muscles too

- Captain Cuckoo with his juggling seals – it's a pity they're afraid of the water!

Steiff's showpieces now have a long tradition. Today the Giengen-based company still maintains a 'showpiece department', which is mainly in charge of developing and assembling the popular displays (see page 132 for further information).

Fig. 146: Albert Schlopsnies and his showpiece 'Steiff Circus'.

Albert Schlopsnies, who had a small 'cabaret shop' (today this would be called a craft shop) in Munich, did not just design the showpieces. His creative ideas can be traced through all areas of the company's advertising. The cover of the Steiff catalogue from 1911, for example, was also his design.

Unfortunately it is no longer possible today to establish clearly whether or not Schlopsnies was also active in the area of product development for a longer period of time. It seems, however, rather improbable that he himself was active for Steiff as a developer after the 'Steiff-Schlopsnies dolls' of the 1920s, which were not entirely successful. It is very likely, though, that he at least influenced product development with his showpiece creations. The following passage from a letter from Richard Steiff on 28th July 1923 seems to confirm this:

If the Schlopsnies dolls don't yield a profit, then let's get rid of them. They're not especially my favourites. ... I never believed in the success of the doll's head by Schlopsnies, but I assumed that others would know better. I can't even remember one piece by Schlopsnies. Nevertheless, his art is very valuable to us, especially here [AUTHOR'S NOTE: IN THE US] where at all costs one must stand out in a crowd. ... And I will only allow such valuable assistance to be used for work that brings us profit.

THE PRE-WAR PERIOD

The catalogue from 1911 is not just interesting because of its new cover design. In the introduction one can also read that Steiff once again won the grand prize at the World's Fair in Brussels in 1910 as it had six years previously in St Louis. This is followed by an inventory of products. And there is further progress to be noted here, for representatives have been appointed in "Amsterdam, Berlin, Brussels, Bucharest, Düsseldorf, Florence, Hamburg, Copenhagen, Leipzig, Lisbon, London, Moscow, New York, Paris, Sydney and Vienna". This gave Margarete Steiff GmbH a presence in almost all of the important metropolises of the world in 1911.

Otto Steiff had been responsible for foreign distribution and for the inventory of samples since the death of Franz Steiff (1908). After building up a mail-order stock in London in 1908-1909, the French branch was founded in 1911. The 1930 anniversary publication reports on this:

... the enormous demand made his stay in London and the building up of a mail-order warehouse there necessary. ... In addition, the branch Steiff Frères Paris was founded in 1911, thereby extending the network of warehouses further across the globe.

Fig. 147: The Steiff catalogue from 1911. The cover was designed by Albert Schlopsnies.

Fig. 148: A page from the introduction of the 1911 catalogue.

The Steiff brothers have always kept an open mind toward all technical innovation. And naturally, they are the first in their hometown to drive motorbikes and cars and the first to use lorries for business. Of course, in Giengen and the rural area then surrounding it, that caused a sensation. On 6th October 1902, Richard wrote the following to his brother Paul:

Fig. 149: Paul Steiff presents himself proudly to the photographers as a chauffeur.

> *Franz drives his Neckarsulm motorbike M600 morning, noon, and night – one-and-three-quarter horsepower; I find how fast it goes uncanny, and it leaves such a stinking cloud of dust behind it that the farmers think the devil is coming to get them.*

With the coming of the new automotive technology the house of Steiff immediately came up with ideas for new products. In 1912 a wide assortment of car accessories was already being offered: headlight covers, radiator mascots, radiator and foot warmers – their imagination was boundless.

106

MARGARETE STEIFF G. M. B. H. GIENGEN-BRENZ (WÜRTTBG.)

Telephon No. 12 ▣ Telegramme: Spielwaren Giengenbrenz ▣ 100 Elektromotoren ▣ 18000 qm Fabrikräume.

Fabrik weichgestopfter Spieltiere, Charakter- und Karikaturpuppen und Roloplan-Drachen

Preisgekrönt auf allen beschickten Ausstellungen ♦ **Schutzmarke Knopf im Ohr** ♦ Grand Prix St. Louis 1904 und Brüssel 1910

Automobil-Tiere und Figuren.

Auto-Schimpanse 9/5322 mit Automütze M. 5.40 Verhindert Hochspritzen von heißem Kühlwasser.

Auto-Schimpanse bei offener Motorhaube oder beim Kühlwasserzugießen, zugleich Kleiderschutz bei heißem oder schmutzigem Kühler.

Auto-Schimpanse 9/5317 mit Automütze und **Steuerrad** aus Messing oder vernickelt M. 7.25

Auch Bär, auf Kühler sitzend — Bär, am Ueberlaufrohr des Kühlers kletternd

Auto-Bär 5317 M. 2.20

Auto-Elefant 5222 M. 4.—

Auto-Esel 5228 M. 3.75

Auto-Glückschwein 8328/2 M. 7.25

Fig. 150: The cover of a four-page catalogue featuring animals and figures for the car from the year 1913.

Auto-Känguru 5235 M. 4.75 (ohne Schnüre)

Auto-Foxterrier 3335 M. 5.85

Auto-Pudel 4335 H M. 6.35

Die Tiere sind mit an den Füßen eingezogenen Schnüren versehen zum Festbinden an der Füllschraube des Automobilkühlers.

No. 268 — 2000 — VII. 13.

Autokühler-Wärmer M. 30.— bis 70.— auch als Fuss-Wärmer zu benützen.

In Filz oder Plüsch. Farbe und Größe nach Angabe. Anweisung zum Massnehmen auf Verlangen.

Fig. 151: Radiator and foot warmers were also produced individually on request.

At the end of 1912 Otto Steiff travelled to the US on behalf of the company, with the aim of increasing the turnover in New York. During his stay, the New York branch was founded. The 1930 anniversary publication contains the following passage:

> *In 1912 he organised a branch in New York called Margarete Steiff & Co. Inc., which turned out to be a reliable and energetic distribution agent for Steiff wares.*

In fact, the house of Steiff had cause to be satisfied on all fronts. The ever-increasing palette of products was accepted well by the customers, the domestic market flourished, and well-organised foreign branches and representatives worked efficiently, with turnover to match. However, the Steiff company and those associated with it would not remain untouched by the looming catastrophe of World War I. Shortly before the outbreak of World War I, on 6th June 1914, Otto Steiff married Johanna Ziegler (born 30th September 1893), the daughter of Karl Albert Ziegler and his wife Hermine Ernestine (née Glatz).

Fig. 152: Otto Steiff and his wife Johanna. Their wedding took place shortly before the outbreak of World War I.

STEIFF DURING WORLD WAR I

World War I raged in Europe, the Middle East, Africa, and Asia from 1914 until 1918 and claimed more than nine million lives. At the beginning, the 'Central Powers', consisting of the 'German Kaiserreich' and Austria-Hungary, fought against the 'Triple Entente', consisting of France, Britain and Russia, plus Serbia. During the course of the war, the Central Powers were completed by the Ottoman Empire and Bulgaria, while the Allies were strengthened by Italy, Portugal, Romania and the US. By the end of the great conflict 25 countries and their colonies were in a state of war – affecting a total of 1.35 billion people, or almost one-quarter of the entire world population at the time.

Nor was the Steiff family exempted from the war and family members were put to its service. Paul Steiff was drafted to the militia and put to work in the sound ranging units 37 and 7 on the French and Macedonian fronts. Richard Steiff, as a veteran of the 127th (the unit where he had previously served his military time), went into action with his motor vehicle when the war broke out. At the beginning he served in the medical convoy, then he was transferred to the motor vehicle park in Diedenhofen where he directed its repair workshops.

Fig. 153: Paul, Richard, Hugo and Otto
Steiff in uniform. They came through World
War I almost without injury.

Hugo Steiff went into action only a short few weeks after the birth of his son Friedrich (born on 20th June 1914) and fought in the war without interruption until the beginning of 1918 on various fronts in France, such as the Priester Forest of the Lorraine region and the Somme River. Regardless of the many hard battles in which he took part, he came home safe and sound, except for a few minor injuries, and with an Iron Cross grades one and two.

Otto Steiff was drafted to the militia in Ulm in December 1914. There he received military training. In December 1915 he went into action with the Esslingen VIII/18 militia battalion which mainly served at the front in the Vosges Mountains. Except for a knee and foot injury that he sustained marching back to Münsingen, he also returned to his home in good health in December 1918.

So, fortunately, the four brothers survived the terrible war in good health except for minor injuries and returned to their workplaces at Margarete Steiff GmbH in 1918. During the war years, the two holders of general power of attorney, Leonhard Meck and Simon Rabus, managed the company. The 1930 anniversary publication reported:

... if the four years of war were survived relatively well that was above all thanks to the two holders of general power of attorney, Leonhard Meck and Simon Rabus. They

109

Margarete Steiff G. m. b. H. Giengen a. Brenz, Württ.

Briefe: Steiff Spielwaren Giengen a. Brenz.   Telegramme: Spielwaren Giengenbrenz.   Fernsprecher: Amt Giengen a. Brenz Nr. 12.   Postscheckkonto Stuttgart 185.

26/6622,0   M. 6.50.   20/1628   M. 18.—.   12/5622   M. 14.—.   12/1628   M. 17.50.

S7/612 5 E   M. 4.—.   36/1614 ex   M. 6.—.   36/2610   M. 2.75.   44/2612   M. 4.50.   44/1614 ex   M. 4.50.   18/1620 ex   M. 8.—.

Weichgestopfte Steiff-Spielwaren aus Ersatzstoffgewebe

Die eingesetzten Preise sind Ladenpreise für Deutschland.

No. 328.   6. 19.

Fig. 154: The front of the colour brochure from June 1919 with "stuffed Steiff toys made of alternative fabrics".

Fig. 155: Today, the Teddy bears made from alternative materials are the most sought-after rarities.

steered the company through this difficult time, with its shortages of labour and materials, having to use replacement material with remarkable talent and prudence. ... After the initial shock and depressive moods following the declaration of war had been overcome, foreign business had decreased but was still satisfactory. Until the beginning of 1916 many goods were taken to America via Holland. It was a difficult time with all the reliable master craftsmen and workers gone, with only this one or that one being free for a few weeks at a time. The company had quickly adjusted to the war by introducing new products. Soldiers in grey uniforms with field equipment proved popular, as did children's military hats and equipment, first-aid dogs, and so on. The animal collection changed little throughout the war, but production numbers had shrunk severely due to the lack of raw materials.

What "shrunk severely" actually means for the company is illustrated by one simple number taken from one of the production lists of these years: in 1918 only 133,937 Steiff products were produced.

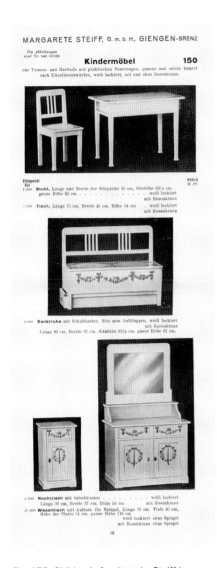

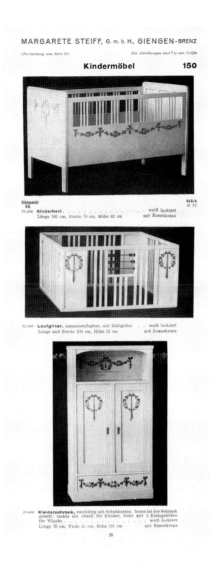

Fig. 157: Painted white, with or without a rose wreath pattern, Steiff's children's furniture moved with the times.

Fig. 156: Children's furniture by Steiff is first shown in the catalogue of 1920.

AFTER THE WAR

When the war broke out, the company had in its employment 800 people, as well as an additional 400 homeworkers. The sales organisation had branches and representatives in almost every country of the northern hemisphere. Now, after the war, it was hard to make ends meet. Raw materials were scarce or just not available, and there was no cash to import necessary materials, especially mohair. Whilst materials for toy animals were short, wood was plentiful so the manufacture of block sets and children's furniture made up for some of the lost production. Textiles which were unavailable were replaced by paper.

In 1919, several simple flyers were distributed, all printed on both sides. Under the headline "New Wooden Toys 1919", "see-sawing animals on eccentric wheels, Steiff building block sets, bows and arrows, and Steiff Drills" were offered in April. The latter was a "flying propeller". On the back "toy animals made from alternative materials" were presented. In June a full-colour brochure was published, this time featuring only "stuffed Steiff toys made from alternative fabrics". "We only use alternative materials of the highest finish and quality. The shape and finish are the same as on our real stuffed toys." This was the statement in the 1919 brochure, where wooden furniture was also offered for the first time. The range comprised a table, chair, bench, child's bed, night table, wardrobe, a washstand with room for a mirror, and a playpen.

In the catalogue of 1920, which once again comprised 20 pages of products, the children's furniture was pictured for the first time. To be on the safe side, however, the following restriction was put into the catalogues and price lists of that year:

This list contains articles that we expect to be available. Given the current difficulties in obtaining raw materials, however, we have to reserve the right to cancel delivery of certain items or to change construction.

In 1921 Margarete Steiff GmbH brought out another interesting and successful new product: 'Skiro' and 'Skirit' are the "Steiff road racers". Hidden behind these names were a wood scooter and a little, foldaway wooden bicycle.

The company made every conceivable effort during these years to make up for the setbacks and losses sustained throughout the war. These efforts included the founding of the Alligator-Ventilfabrik (Alligator Valve Factory) as a department of Margarete Steiff GmbH (see page 165). Production numbers actually increased with this. At any rate, three times as many Steiff products were manufactured in 1921 as in 1918. However, business results continued to be unsatisfactory and the company was doing exceptionally poorly economically.

The cause for this company crisis lay – how could it be otherwise? – in the war and its disastrous effects for the entire economy. The gigantic state deficit caused by the war and the galloping inflationary currency depreciation in the post-war era had disastrous effects. In 1920 the mark, measured against the dollar, was only worth a tenth of what it had been worth in August of 1914, in July 1922 only a hundredth, and in October of the same year only a thousandth. The depreciation of the mark against the US dollar went ever more quickly until finally the inflation peaked in November 1923 when one US dollar could be bought for 4.2 trillion marks. This hyperinflation finally led to the breakdown of the entire German economy. Only the currency reform of 1923, as well as generous American credits (the Dawes Plan of 1924), ended the process of economic decline, making possible the economic recovery that finally lead to a time of prosperous upswing – the 'Golden Twenties'.

However, it is obvious what the inflation and the breakdown of the economy meant for Margarete Steiff GmbH, a company that bought the lion's share of its raw materials abroad with foreign currencies. Within the country's borders money

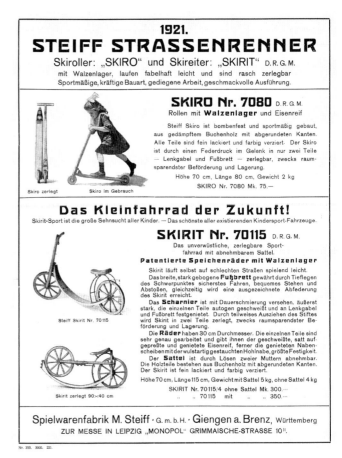

Fig. 158: Scooters were included in the Steiff programme from 1921.

Fig. 159: Richard Steiff, portrayed here in a painting, emigrated to the US in 1923 with his family.

was now cheap. The time was ideal for investment. And Steiff made good use of the favourable timing. Various construction measures were completed in 1923. The two bridges joining the west and north buildings were added; the vault building on the north-east side of the north building and the large Brenz bridge, which once would be the main factory gate and makes possible direct access to the railway.

The problem during this period was getting hold of foreign currencies; it was almost impossible to get financing for this. The anniversary publication of 1955, marking the 75th anniversary of the company, mentioned getting credit in dollars, with which the company could finally begin importing the necessary raw materials once more. This is confirmed by a letter from Richard Steiff from 6th January 1931:

The truth is that in all these years I achieved more cash profits here [AUTHOR'S NOTE: IN THE US] *for the limited company than the company itself* [AUTHOR'S NOTE: IN GERMANY]. *Apart from that I also procured vital credits.*

Richard Steiff, who emigrated to the US with his family in 1923, proved once again how important he was for Margarete Steiff GmbH. This time it was not a creation, however, which benefited the company, but the procurement of that "vital" credit.

Richard Steiff wrote letters from the US almost daily. He wanted to be informed precisely of all activities in Giengen. Above all, he gave exact instructions on improving the current range and expressed ideas for new products. On 7th August 1923, for example, he sent drawings and instructions for some of his new ideas, among them "jumping toys, clockwork toys, and walking toys". In the accompanying letter he spelt out what he wanted very clearly:

I hope this won't need many months of brooding in the prototype department ... I'm here to create profitable work for you. There's no need to get upset when my suggestions make a lot more urgent and fulfilling work for you – on the other hand I'm also eradicating thankless tasks. Even if not everyone likes it! ... The prototype room needs to report to me constantly on what it's doing! This way time won't be wasted with the wrong stuff like it has up to now.

THE TAYLOR SYSTEM AND PRODUCTION LINE ASSEMBLY

Richard Steiff was very self-confident. He knew precisely what he wanted. When it came to the quality of Steiff products he was not prepared to compromise in any way. And when something didn't go according to his plan, his choice of words in correspondence to his siblings was not always overly sensitive. This is illustrated by a passage from a letter of 28th July 1923:

> *The most important factor is perfect good taste. That, however, doesn't count for anything in the Taylor System since it can't be measured with a stopwatch. This important factor – which is what wins us our contracts – is completely eliminated by the pure production system. Hugo's 'system' must not have absolute power. It will never mean anything without a continual improvement in the beauty of the products...I have never doubted the true importance of rational work and production methods, and especially their execution, but I have to doubt the sanity of anyone who does not think my creative activity is just as important. I require an according explanation from the directors, regarding the pronouncements made during and after the last general assembly. Otherwise I will regard them as arch enemies of myself and the company and act accordingly.*

Fig. 160: Hugo Steiff, here testing the endurance of two wheeled animals. His opinion of the Taylor System differed greatly from that of his brother Richard Steiff.

The subject of these expressions is the so-called 'Taylor System' introduced by Hugo Steiff. In his book, *The Principles of Scientific Management*, the American engineer and economist Frederick Winslow Taylor (1856-1915) expressed the opinion that the main problem of companies in his day lay in the wasting of human work capacity. According to him, inefficient work structures, as well as most managers' unsatisfactory understanding of efficient production processes, were responsible for this deplorable state of affairs. The first step in fighting the causes for wasting human work capacity lay, according to the Taylor System, in undertaking time-and-motion studies. All of the work done in the company was documented down to the last detail, then analysed minutely as to how and with how many tools workers did their work and in what amount of time. Analysis of the data gathered allowed the management to determine the most efficient methods and the most suitable personnel for any given work process.

Hugo Steiff used this Taylor System to prepare for the introduction of production line assembly. It was Hugo who finally won the argument with his brother Richard

Fig. 161: Hugo Steiff introduced production line assembly at Steiff in 1925.

over the pros and cons of this type of production system. In 1925 the first Steiff product to come off the production line was manufactured, the Steiff scooter. The system remained reliable and was applied to further products. The 1930 anniversary publication commented on this progress in production methods:

> *The company's preparation and execution of a switch over to production line assembly was Mr Hugo Steiff's work. The Steiff scooter was moved to the production line first, making this piece unimaginably cheaper, and so increasing turnover. At the end of 1925 this system – which saved on time, energy and storage – was extended to the stuffed animals, entailing a partial change in work preparation. The most important thing was that the need for great stocks of half-finished articles in varying work processes ended; this had the effect of freeing up large storage rooms and meant large quantities could be pushed through quickly.*

115

Fig. 162: 'Molly', the new product for 1925, remained in the Steiff range until 1969.

Fig. 163: Also added to the Steiff range in 1925: 'Teddy Rosé'.

With the introduction of production line work the entire company was rationalised little by little. Furthermore, products were matched to the tastes of the times, making the range appear more modern. Since 1925, Steiff animals made of mohair had been fashionable. Dogs were the most popular. 'Molly', a "young, soft puppy made of long-haired mohair plush" became a hit. And more colour was being added to the game: pink, yellow, red, blue – there were no limits to the imagination. In 1927, 1,000,000 Steiff articles were produced again for the first time since 1907.

Also in this year, Ernst Steiff returned to the family company after a 14-year absence and a very eventful time in the US. After ending his apprenticeship at Steiff, he did military service at the Royal Bavarian Detachment in Munich, after which he attended the Technical Rhine School in Bingen. In December 1913 he travelled to the US with the goal of consolidating his education as an electrical engineer. There he worked first at Hans Motor Equipment Co. in La Crosse, Wisconsin.

The outbreak of the war prevented him from returning home as the British navy had blockaded the Atlantic. In the spring of 1915 he visited the German Methodist College in Berea, Ohio. The same year he travelled to the World's Fair in San Francisco and then on to Lake Geneva, Wisconsin. There he visited the YMCA's summer school. Returning to La Crosse, he built ploughing machines for La Crosse Tractor Co., then steam-heating instruments for Trane & Co. From 1921 to 1922 he was a lay preacher at the German Methodist Church in Tomah, Wisconsin.

He finally returned home at the end of 1927. There, on 3rd May 1928, he married Sophie Josenhans (born 14th April 1897), the daughter of Robert Heinrich Josenhans and his wife Luise Karoline (née Schuster). Ernst Steiff worked at Margarete Steiff GmbH as a technician, the profession he had learned. In 1929 he received a general commercial power of attorney.

116

Fig. 164: A Steiff family reunion in 1927.

Fig. 165: Ernst Steiff and his wife Sophie.
The wedding took place on 3rd May 1928,
after his return from the US.

THE WORLD ECONOMIC CRISIS

The 'Golden Twenties' came to an abrupt end toward the close of the decade. Various factors led to a breakdown of the economy in all leading industrial nations. The day of the collapse of the stock market in the US – 24th October 1929 – is commonly hailed as the beginning of the world economic crisis. During World War I, the US, South America and various colonies had strongly increased their production levels in order to satisfy the demand of European countries which couldn't produce anything themselves due to the war. When production started up again in Europe, there was a surplus of goods – and the markets reacted with falling prices.

The situation in the stock market was comparable. For months, there had been a bull market like no other before. Many people had taken out credit in order to participate in the boom. When prices which had been speculatively overvalued began

117

to fall, they couldn't meet the credit payments any longer and had to sell, a fact that pushed prices down even further. The result – on 25th October 1929 – was Black Friday, the beginning of a sharp fall in prices of up to 90 per cent, which lasted for more than three years. Such destruction of capital inevitably led to another set-back in investments, decreasing consumption and sinking prices – the classic elements of deflation.

Mass unemployment and a massive decrease in world trade were the dramatic results of the world economic crisis. In the German Reich there were 1.4 million unemployed in 1929; in February of 1930 there were 3.5 million, and 5 million already at the end of 1930. The politicians' attempt to get the crisis under control by strengthening the Reichsmark combined with making drastic cuts in social services failed. In February 1932 there were 6.12 million unemployed on the streets in Germany. Only 12 million people still had a job.

Of course, the world economic crisis had a dramatic effect on Steiff's balance sheets. Production levels sunk to 197,209 pieces in 1933, after reaching more than a million a year in 1927 and in 1928.

The company's anniversary took place right in the middle of the world economic crisis in 1930. "Fifty years of Steiff toys" was the motto of the anniversary publication so often quoted in this book, one that carries an exceptionally optimistic tone considering the times:

Fig. 166: A celebratory parade was organised on the occasion of the company's 50th anniversary.

We also want to look forward, and not only back, taking control of our new tasks just as happily and continuing to develop our work just as organically as our founder taught us. Children all over the globe can expect that their childhoods will continue to be brightened by Steiff toys – including 'Button in Ear', the sign of quality.

THE 1930S AND WORLD WAR II

The catastrophic economic situation also encouraged the rise of National Socialism in Germany. On 30th January 1933 Hitler was named Reich Chancellor by Reich President Paul von Hindenburg. The house of Steiff had successfully overcome all the crises of the last three decades: the American economic crisis of 1907, World War I, and the ensuing breakdown of the entire economy. The world economic crisis prevailing at the time would also be overcome. But what did this radically changed political situation within the German Reich mean for Steiff?

Hitler and his regime were clearly on a course of looming international confrontation; this naturally created a great deal of mistrust not only in Europe, but also in the US and many parts of the rest of the world. Steiff was now also beginning to feel the increasing resentment against Germany (and German products). For years Steiff had been consistently building up its business in the US, and had not only conquered a new market, but had also made an excellent name for itself and garnered excellent contacts. Thanks to the commitment of Geo. Borgfeld & Co., the company responsible for the distribution of Steiff's products in the US since 1913, Steiff had even manufactured the two original American cartoon stars Mickey and Minnie Mouse for Walt Disney. But with the rise to power of the National Socialists, this co-operation, begun in 1931, was already at an end by 1934. The production of Mickey and Minnie had to be stopped. Even remnant stock was no longer accepted, and, after 1936, it became available on the German market as 'clearance goods' for this reason.

The 1930s weren't only years of economic change for Steiff. Drastic restructuring was taking place among the staff,

Fig. 167: Mickey and Minnie Mouse, American cartoon legends, may not be manufactured anymore by Steiff after 1934.

119

mainly because of the changed political situation in Germany. Hugo Steiff left the management. Due to his long stay to the US and his closeness to the church, Ernst Steiff was denounced by the National Socialists. He had to leave the company and was periodically imprisoned by the Nazis. Paul Steiff remained a registered managing director, but worked almost exclusively on the creation of new prototypes. It was Otto Steiff who, above all, manoeuvred the company through these difficult years, for even Richard Steiff could no longer take control of the company management from the US. On 30th March 1939, only a few weeks after his 62nd birthday, Richard Steiff died of a heart attack in Jackson, Michigan. With his death, Margarete Steiff GmbH lost its most creative innovator and the worldwide toy industry one of its most experienced and committed representatives. In his obituary, the following was printed:

Fig. 168: Otto Steiff managed the company through the 1930s and during World War II until his death on 21st February 1944.

We are in deep mourning over the news of the sudden death of our esteemed director and the co-founder of our company Mr Richard Steiff in Jackson, Michigan, USA. In the dearly departed, we lose an excellent leader of our company. His untiring power to create, his far-sighted business visions, his rich knowledge in artistic and technical areas, his true and honourable character are what we have to thank for the success of our company from modest beginnings. He was always striving toward the success of his work and the well-being of his employees. The memories of the departed will live on in our hearts and his name will remain indelible in the history of our company.

On 1st September 1939, five months after the death of Richard Steiff, World War II began. With the outbreak of the war, the toy company's activities had to be strongly reined back. Most of the male personnel were drafted for war service, and materials were hard to come by. In 1943 the mohair material finally ran out for good. The activities of Margarete Steiff GmbH finally came to a full stop, for no one wanted the animals made with the alternative material, 'artificial silk plush'. Toys were simply not popular during this difficult time.

In 1944, Otto Steiff died on 21st February, followed on 26th December by Maria Blickle, Margarete Steiff's youngest niece and one of the limited partners. Georg Köpff, the husband of Margarete's favourite niece Eva, succeeded Otto Steiff as managing director in 1944.

FROM THE ECONOMIC MIRACLE UNTIL TODAY

At the end of the war Giengen, and the Steiff factory, were both located in the American zone. The factory had come through the war without damage, but there were hardly any trained personnel. Due to the lack of materials and the unheated production rooms, restarting production could only be achieved with improvisation and a lot of goodwill. As during the war, animals were now being manufactured with alternative materials; wooden pieces were also being made, such as the cradle wagon, for example, or the Steiff 'Corso', a collapsible pram. The 1955 anniversary publication describes the modest post-war production thus:

> *Directly after the war only artificial silk plush was available, exclusively targeted for the export programme, which was just beginning. At the Leipzig Fair in 1946 and 1947 the company only put ten products out for sale.*

Fig. 169 below left: A flyer from 1947 for the Steiff 'Corso', a collapsible pram.

Fig. 170 below right: The first Steiff catalogue after World War II was published in 1948 and contained only animals made of artificial silk plush.

In 1948 the first eight-page, illustrated catalogue was published, containing only animals made of artificial silk plush. On 20th June of the same year, the so-called Trizone region (the amalgamation of the American, British and French zones) implemented a currency reform, introducing the 'DM' (Deutschmark). Because of this, the western part of Germany quickly experienced an economic upturn. On 23rd May 1949, the Federal Republic of Germany was finally founded, followed by the founding of the German Democratic Republic on 7th October 1949.

After the currency reform, Steiff also experienced an upward trend. The 1955 anniversary publication reports:

> *In 1948, a commission finishing deal with Switzerland finally brought the opportunity of obtaining the essential mohair material. It was just impossible to sell artificial silk animals abroad. ... At the first German exhibition in New York in 1949, Steiff's sales director could finally present a worthy collection once again.*

Fig. 171: Karl Vallendor and his wife. He contributed greatly to the rebuilding of Steiff after World War II.

The sales director who represented Steiff in the US in 1949 was Karl Vallendor. In 1930, still director of advertising, he had written that year's anniversary publication. He received general commercial power of attorney and, together with Ernst Steiff (who became managing director in 1949), contributed greatly to rebuilding the limited company.

At the trade fairs, the company also presented something new. For decades, Leipzig had been for Steiff – as well as for other toy manufacturers – the grand shopwindow and meeting place for producers and customers in Germany and abroad. From 1949 this role was taken over by the German Toy Fair that has been held annually since then in Nuremberg.

On 22nd July 1950 Georg Köpff passed away. Soon thereafter, management was once again supplemented, with the next generation following in the footsteps of its ancestors. Hans-Otto Steiff, son of Otto Steiff and great-nephew of Margarete, began working at the company on 1st September 1950 as company secretary after successfully receiving his diploma in engineering. On 1st March 1951 he was promoted to the managerial floor.

Fitting with the company's upward development, in 1951 the cornerstone for the next great sale success was laid. 'Mecki', the hedgehog figure, became very popular with the general public thanks to appearances in the television magazine *Hör Zu*. Margarete Steiff GmbH manufactured it under license of Gebrüder Diehl, together with its hedgehog family, 'Micki', 'Macki' and 'Mucki'.

The turnover numbers achieved by the 'Mecki' family were so great that at the company the 1950s were also called the 'Mecki years'. It was very similar to the time around 1907 when 'Teddy' became the star.

Also in the US, thanks to good relations from the time before World War II, Steiff again found success. Bambi, Walt Disney's fawn, was manufactured by Steiff from 1951 under Disney's copyright. Further Disney animals, such as the squirrel 'Perry', soon followed. Reeves International, Inc. in New Jersey was awarded the exclusive distribution rights for Steiff products in the US.

Fig. 172: 'Mecki', the hedgehog figure, was a great success from 1951 on.

Fig. 173: From 1951 Steiff manufactured Walt Disney's fawn Bambi under copyright.

Fig. 174 right: Walt Disney, surrounded by Steiff animals.

Fig. 175: Celebrations in Giengen on the occasion of the
100th birthday of Theodore 'Teddy' Roosevelt in 1958.

Fig. 176: Paul Steiff was employed by Steiff from
1898 until his death in 1954.

Completely unexpectedly, Ernst Steiff died on 21st March 1953, three days before his 63rd birthday. The following year three of his siblings followed him: Hugo Steiff on 3rd May, Lina Leo on 20th September, and Paul Steiff on 26th September 1954. Of Margarete Steiff's nine nieces and nephews, only Eva Köpff remained. When she died on 3rd June 1965, she was the last representative of the generation that had once personally inherited the company from its founder. After the deaths of managing directors Ernst and Paul, only Hans-Otto Steiff still represented the family name in the company's management.

The company's rapid growth also increased the need for more room. After some minor construction work in 1950, three years later a new three-storey building for toy production was built. The employee numbers also mirrored this positive development. The number of people working for Steiff increased from about 985 in January 1948 to 1,811 in 1954.

The next year was finally one of celebration once again. The company's 75th anniversary was celebrated under the motto "the cradle of the Teddy bear". And only three years later the 100th birthday of Theodore Roosevelt, famous among other things for giving his name to the Teddy bear, was celebrated in Giengen with a Teddy festival and a great parade through the streets. Visitors came from all over the world, marking the fact that the company had once more arrived. The time of isolation was finally over.

In order to be able to deal with the increased volume of contracts, a factory branch for production was put up in Höchstädt a.d. Donau. Steiff animals were made there until the shut down in 1996.

124

Fig. 178: 'Dolan-Zotty' was manufactured from 1970 until 1976 at the Grieskirchen factory.

Fig. 177: Hans-Otto Steiff managed Margarete Steiff GmbH for more than thirty years.

In the 1960s and 1970s the range was greatly extended. To match the tastes of the period, many new shapes and materials were introduced. Better safety standards were also established: 'non flammable', 'non-poisonous', and 'washable' were just some of the characteristics of the new quality and safety policy. Because of increasing market globalisation, price played an ever more important role. New production technology and further rationalisation aided this development.

There were also changes in management during these years. Friedhelm Steiff was promoted to the managerial floor in 1970, a position that he fulfilled until 1974 when he left the company. In September of 1970, Hans-Otto Steiff was named sole managing director, a function he also executed for sister companies Alligator Ventilfabrik GmbH and Steiff Förder- und Automatisierungstechnik. His commitment stretched far beyond this position, however. As long-standing chairman of the board of the International Toy Fair in Nuremberg and the Giengener Volksbank eG bank, president of the Chamber of Commerce of East Württemberg, chairman of the Industry Association 'Spiel + Hobby' (Play + Hobby), and simultaneously chairman of the Association of the German Toy Industry and board and committee member for various associations and banks, he asserted his influence for Margarete Steiff GmbH and continued to build upon the company's important position. Due to his great services to the German economy, he received the order of the Federal Republic of Germany first class in 1979 and the order of Bavaria in 1983. From 1981 until 31st December 1984 Hans-Otto Steiff was the sole managing director of Steiff Beteiligungsgesellschaft mbH. In 1985 he left the company (please see chapter I for details on the family's participation in the company's management thereafter.) His decisions to point the way and great deeds for the company and home town were honoured in 1989 when he was given the freedom of the city of Giengen. On 31st December 1994 Hans-Otto Steiff passed away.

Fig. 179: 'Papa Bear' appeared in 1980 as the first limited edition of an historical Steiff product.

There was another great celebration for the 100th anniversary of Steiff in 1980. On the occasion of this historical event a new product idea was introduced: old designs were reproduced as close to the original as possible and manufactured in limited editions. The first example of this type, 'Papa Bear', was issued in a limited edition of 11,000 and was sold worldwide. He kicked off an exceptionally successful series, which is still important today, especially for collectors. In the basement level of the east building from 1903 the first Steiff Museum opened. There, a colourful cross-section of products from 100 years of Steiff's history is on show. In recent history there have been two grand Steiff celebrations of note: the 150th birthday of founder Margarete Steiff in 1997 and the 100th anniversary of the Teddy bear three years ago.

125

Fig. 181: To celebrate the 150th birthday of
Margarete Steiff in 1997 a large festival featuring many attractions was put on in Giengen.

Fig. 180: The first Steiff museum was opened in the anniversary year 1980 under the name 'Margarete Steiff Museum'.

OUTLOOK

In the future, the company philosophy of Margarete Steiff GmbH – true to its 125-year tradition – will continue to centre upon children and children's rooms throughout the world. The product range will tap into all areas, from furniture to clothing and, of course, toys. And, naturally, adults won't be forgotten. The exceptionally successful collector's market will continue to be catered for and supported just as the beloved and popular Steiff animal will continue to retain its place in the product range for 'big people'. Without doubt, the fact that 90 per cent of Germans recognise the Steiff name is a great achievement. But the trust placed in the quality of the brand also represents an obligation for the future.

Fig. 182: The musical 'Teddy' (author and director: Uli Brée) was staged in 2002 to honour Richard Steiff's creation.

127

From toy to collector's item

THE PRODUCTS

Fig. 183: Margarete Steiff's seal including the elephant chosen to become the trademark – a quality guarantee for every single product from the history of the 125-year-old company.

Fig. 184: German patent certificate from 16th July 1909 for "toy animals with a movable head".

Great brand names like Rosenthal, Beiersdorf, and Bosch – just to name a few – were created around the turn of the twentieth century. The development of the Steiff trademark 'Button in Ear' is a classic example of a German brand history. More than 20 years passed from the appearance of the first 'Elefäntle' to the final incarnation of the clear and unmistakable brand still seen today. During that time a unique product range was built, its manufacture and distribution organised efficiently, and the necessary legal measures taken to protect the still very young, though exceptionally promising and innovative company and its products.

A decisive step, alongside developing the trademark, was to register protective rights for patterns and designs, basically securing legal protection for the company's own inventions and creations (see page 68). There are a lot of beautifully drafted documents and certificates from the founding era to be found in Margarete Steiff GmbH's archives. They give an impression of the toy factory's far-reaching activities and are simultaneously proof of the extraordinary creativity during that time.

Then, as now, advertising was an indispensable marketing instrument in the toy industry. This concept was understood very early at Steiff, and the company used all of the media available at the time to reach its goals. The inherent charm of the articles being publicised went a long way in itself to ensuring the success of any advertising campaign (as is still the case today). Once the interest for a Steiff animal was awakened, many customers were convinced of the products' quality and beauty and were willing to buy.

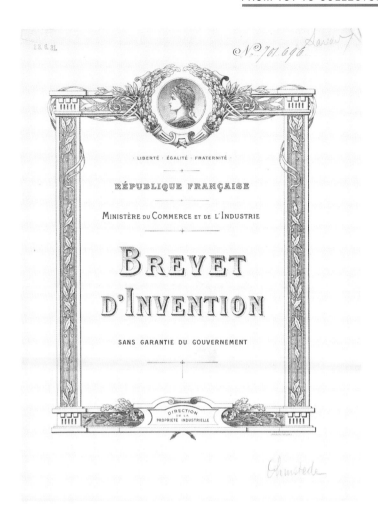

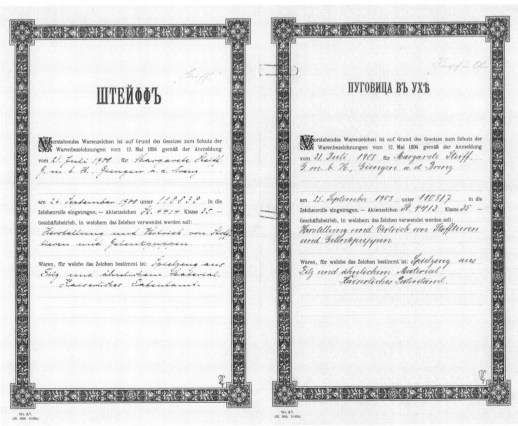

Fig. 185 above left: American patent from 14th September 1909 concerning "joint connections".

Fig. 186 above: French patent certificate from 23rd June 1931.

Fig. 187 left: Registration of the trademarks 'Steiff' and 'Button in Ear' in Russian language.

Fig. 188-190: Various scenes from the
showpiece 'The Great Steiff Circus'.

The showpieces have remained an especially successful and impressive example of
Steiff marketing. They demonstrate the great variety of Steiff's range over the last
125 years as well as their development – something that can of course only be
touched upon here. (For those who may have a more extensive interest in this,
please refer to books already published on the Steiff product ranges.) The mechanical showpiece 'The Great Steiff Circus' (already mentioned in Chapter 4) kicked
this tradition off in 1910 at Berlin's Wertheim department store. In 1911 the same
showpiece was exhibited at the Leipzig Fair.

Fig. 191: Fair showpiece 'Fire Brigade' from 1912.

The presentation of the animals and dolls from each of Steiff's topical ranges could not have been more perfectly put in context than in one of these extensive, large-area showpieces. And Steiff was always exceptionally successful in finding various themes and motifs to present their new programme of products to the public. So it was natural in 1912 for the new firemen in the range to become the subject of the fair showpiece of the same year. The following year 'Noah's Ark' offered the opportunity of presenting a colourful variety of toy animals. The most famous showpiece, 'Städtle' or Little City, was shown at the German Commercial Fair in Munich in 1922 and parts of it at the Leipzig Fair. Its high degree of fame, though, is largely due to Richard Steiff taking it to the USA in 1923, showing it at various opportunities. Only a few years ago parts of it were rediscovered there. Today, they can be seen in Basel's 'Puppenhausmuseum' (Doll's House Museum) after Margarete Steiff GmbH undertook a reconstruction following the original form.

Fig. 192: Noah's Ark' is the topic for this
large showpiece from 1913.

Fig. 193 right: A scene from Wilhelm Busch's
Max and Moritz from 1914.

Fig. 194 outside right: Excerpt from 1922's
'Städtle'.

Fig. 196 above: A design by Helmut Braig from 1953 for the 'Carnival' showpiece.

Fig. 195 left: 'Mecki' figures have often been used in showpieces since the 1950s.

After World War II the showpiece tradition was continued. 'Mecki' became the most popular character alongside the animals of the time. Between 1911 and 1923 in Giengen, Albert Schlopsnies had provided sensational concepts with his humorous ideas for the successful presentation of Steiff showpieces and, from 1949 until 1978, an artist was once again hired to be in charge of many of the creative new developments. Through family contacts Helmut Braig, the very extrovert and unconventional painter and sculptor today famous far beyond the borders

Fig. 197: The fairy tale showpiece 'Once Upon a Time' was shown in 1998 as a large fair showpiece in Nuremberg.

136

Fig. 198: A look inside a moving showpiece.

Fig. 199: Cover from the 'Steiff Advertising Adviser' from 1953.

of Giengen, was persuaded to work for the house of Steiff. His creations were modern and fit well with the styles of the times.

The last great showpieces to be shown at Nuremberg's toy fair were 'Once Upon a Time', 'Journey to the Moon', 'The Underwater World', and '1001 Nights' from 1998 until 2001. Even in modern times Steiff showpieces have lost nothing of their attractiveness and effect on both large and small audiences. But it is not only the large showpieces that cause sensations. Small scenes that fit into the window display of a toy shop are especially popular decorations for Steiff dealers. 'Advertising guides' are also regularly published, containing aids for various advertising methods such as design templates for printed adverts, transparencies for cinema advertising, and decoration suggestions for windows and display cases. Theme worlds with only one type of animal are also popular – such as bears, dogs, cats, or bunnies – and are often also used as motifs for advertising postcards. The smaller showpieces especially, which are produced as part of a series and sold within the regular Steiff programme, are very popular with the public.

Steiff products from the early days of the company right up to the 1950s have long since become exceptionally sought-after antiques and collector's items. At interna-

Fig. 200: Postcard motif from the
1910s. Dogs of varying breeds enjoy
a 'dog restaurant'.

Fig. 201: Decoration scene with a
hurdy-gurdy man and dancing bears
from the mid-1920s.

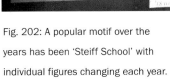

Fig. 202: A popular motif over the years has been 'Steiff School' with individual figures changing each year.

Fig. 203: The Christmas tree motif offers an especially large range of opportunities to present Steiff articles.

Fig. 204: The 'Millennium Carousel' from 2000 kicked off the series of small displays in Steiff's range.

Fig. 205 left: The popular 'Teddy Bear Workshop' was introduced as a new product within the small display series in 2002.

Fig. 206: The black 'Original Teddy' from the 1950s is currently the most expensive Steiff product from the era after 1945, auctioned at a price of 55,800 euros.

Fig. 207: Currently the most expensive Teddy bear in the world: it was sold at the Sixth Steiff Festival's special auction on 29th June 2002 for 156,240 euros.

tional auctions record prices are achieved. The most expensive Teddy bear currently in existence was sold on 29th June 2002 at a special auction during the 6th Steiff Festival for 156,240 euros. This was a 40-centimetre Teddy bear made of brown tipped mohair; only a very small number were manufactured between 1926 and 1927. Presently, the most expensive Steiff animal is the caricature fox terrier 'Bonzo'. This is a prototype of a dog planned for the American market in 1927 that was never manufactured in series; it was also auctioned in 2002 for 61,380 euros. Prices of this magnitude are not only achieved for pre-World War II products. At 55,800 euros a 35-centimetre black bear from the 1950s is fourteenth on the current list of the most expensive Steiff bears and animals of all time.

For more than 20 years the product range has also contained special collector's editions that enjoy great popularity alongside the classic Steiff toys. The series

Fig. 209 left: 'Jackie', the popular anniversary bear from 1953, was offered in three sizes as a limited replica between 1986 and 1990.

Fig. 210 right: The 'Nagano' Teddy bear was produced in a limited edition of 2,500 especially for the Japanese market to mark the occasion of the 1998 Winter Olympics.

Fig. 208: 'Bonzo', a caricature fox terrier is currently the most expensive Steiff animal. It was auctioned in 2002 for a price of 61,380 euros.

beginning with 'Papa Bear' in 1980 gave birth to a very popular independent collector's field. Replicas, museum collections, historical miniatures, country editions and many more have become sought-after objects for many collectors worldwide. And that is mirrored in the prices that are paid on the secondary market for these products. Often the original retail prices are doubled and tripled within a very short amount of time. There are quite a number of articles for which enthusiasts and collectors have paid almost ten times the original retail price.

In the future this area will continue to have a permanent place within the Steiff range as 'Steiff Classic'. The main emphasis will continue to comprise all articles traditionally found in a child's room, arranged in the categories 'Baby' and 'Cosy Friends'. Furniture, accessories, and clothing are produced by other manufacturers under license and round off Steiff's range of products.

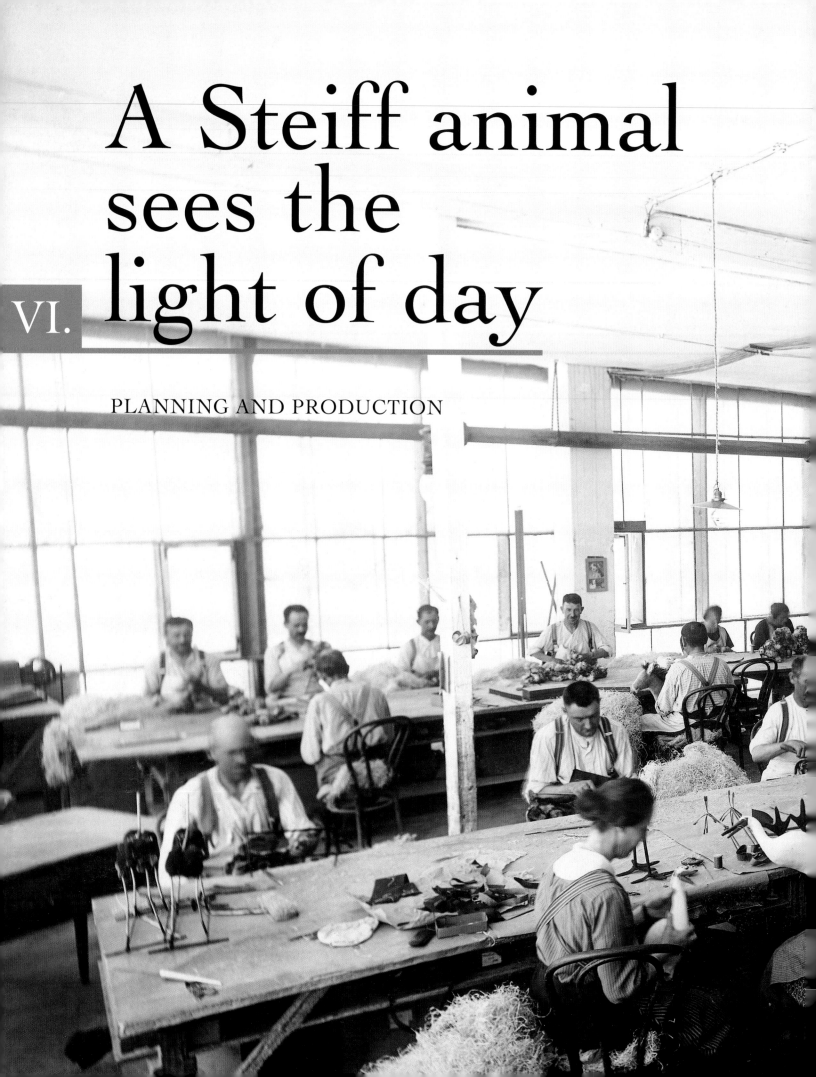

A Steiff animal sees the light of day

PLANNING AND PRODUCTION

Fig. 211: A look into the Steiff production workshop during the 1920s.

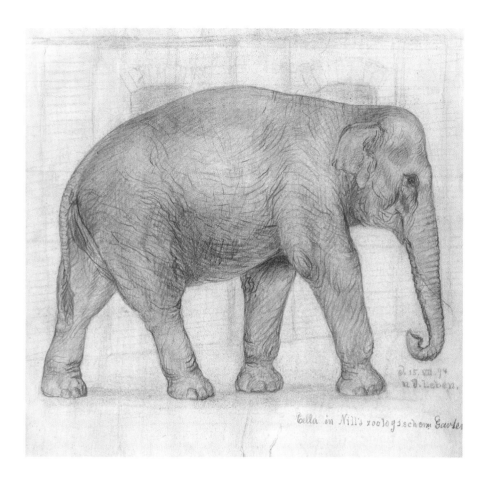

Fig. 212: A drawing from Richard Steiff's sketchbook.

Fig. 213: Elephants in the wild – objects of study for the developers of today.

One hundred and twenty-five years ago, Margarete Steiff manufactured her first felt elephant according to a pattern she found in the magazine *Modenwelt*. The materials she needed were felt, fleece, two 10-centimetre-long, white, bone knitting needles, two black porcelain buttons, a piece of colourful material, and a little silk thread. Needles and scissors were her only tools. Much has changed since then. The materials used have become much more numerous, the tools highly technical specialised machines, and the production process perfectly organised. However, the care and attention to detail that go into manufacturing Steiff animals have remained unchanged to the present day. And the philosophy also once formulated by Margarete Steiff has also remained unchanged to the present day: "For children, only the best is good enough!" Over the last 125

Fig. 214: A Steiff animal that carries the 'hand sample' label is the first approved model of a new piece.

Fig. 215: The so-called 'sample button' was used from about 1910 until the 1930s to denote hand samples.

years, many millions of Steiff animals have been received by happy children and adults and, at such a moment, who stops to think about the many steps necessary to create a perfect Steiff animal? For all those interested not just in the history and aesthetic appeal of the famous Steiff products but also in the techniques used to create them, the following will give you a glimpse into the planning and production processes.

PREPARATION

At first glance it is amazing to see that the original production processes have basically stayed the same, despite all the modern technology and detailed organisation. Design remains the starting-point for it all. More than one hundred years ago, Richard Steiff studied live animals at Stuttgart's Nill Zoo. Today, Steiff's designers travel all the way to Kenya in order to study animals in the wild, for every detail should come as close to nature as possible.

Then they choose the materials. There are, of course, always large stocks of materials in Steiff's warehouse. But frequently special pieces are made; for these, the right materials have first to be manufactured by the suppliers. When all the necessary materials are ready, it's time to head to the prototype department – and that's something that was the same during Richard Steiff's era as well.

By the time the final sample is done, a myriad of different models has been created; each one of these is made completely by hand. Only when the designer is satisfied with the results does he or she present it to a committee comprising employees from various departments; this committee is responsible for finally accepting and adopting the new product. Together with the development department, this committee decides whether the new creation will be added to the Steiff range.

If the decision is positive, the piece created becomes the so-called 'hand sample'. It is given the company trademarks of Steiff button and 'hand sample' ear tag. These two elements confirm that this is the first approved model of a new product. During Richard Steiff's time the hand samples were earmarked with their own 'Musterknopf' (sample button), which was used instead of the Steiff button.

After that, up to ten copies are produced, following this hand sample exactly; these also receive a Steiff button and a special ear tag, though the tag is now printed with the word Werkmuster, or 'type sample'. They later serve each of the departments

Fig. 216: Pattern for cat '606-2 M', which was carried in the Steiff range under this article number from 1899 until 1901.

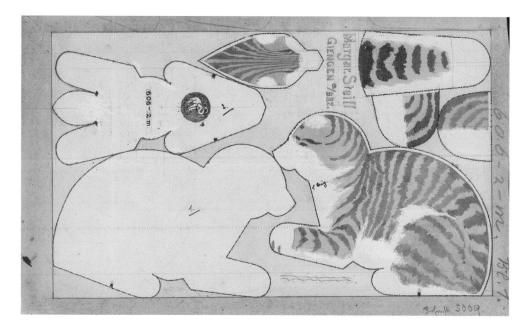

Fig. 217: The same pattern, but this time printed on material.

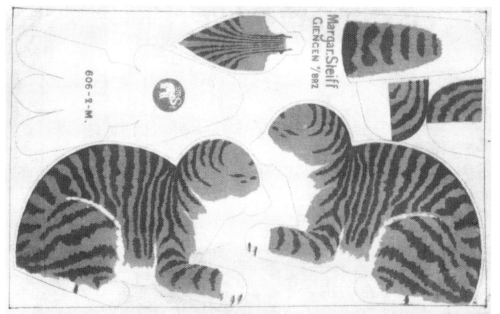

Fig. 218: The lying velvet cat '606-2 M' with its ball of wool is only 10 cm long.

as the model for the individual production steps; the appearance of the prototype may not be altered in any way during production. Then, just as they were 100 years ago, the patterns are created. But what was done tediously by hand in earlier times is now carried out much more quickly and precisely by computer.

Only when the materials have all been delivered by the suppliers, and necessary equipment, such as templates and special tools, is present, production can finally begin. Today, the preparation phase still lasts several months; this fact well explains why Richard Steiff wrote "I hope this won't need many months of brooding in the prototype department" when he sent his suggestions for new products to Giengen from the United States in 1923.

Fig. 219: Steiff's cutting and stamping department in 1924.

Fig. 220: The coloured lines along which the individual parts will be cut can be clearly seen on the back of the mohair.

THE PRODUCTION PROCESS

The actual production begins with the cutting. Different techniques are used for different materials. Felt and velvet, for example, can be stamped out because their piles are very short. Mohair, on the other hand, is cut, so that its longer pile is not damaged. According to the length of the pile and the type of cutting the material needs, it is done either with normal scissors or with an electrically supported, hand-guided cutting machine. However, the weave must also not be damaged during the cutting, otherwise bald spots would later appear at the seams.

If the individual parts are to be cut by hand, the exact shape is reproduced beforehand on the back of the plush. This is done with the aid of a large metal plate. The contours of the individual body parts are transferred to the metal plate by drilling a multitude of small holes. The prepared plate is then laid onto the mohair, which is stretched across long tables and secured in place; paint is then brushed onto it. In this way the contour lines for cutting are made visible on the back side of the plush.

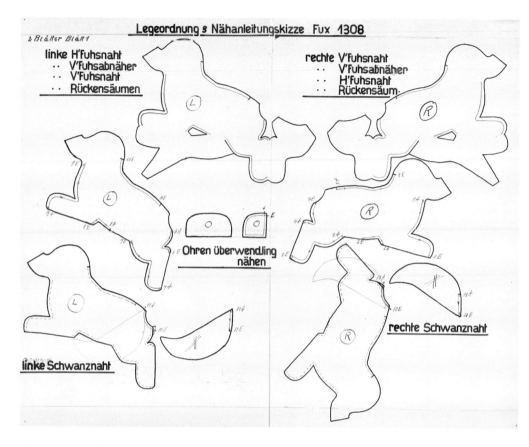

Legeordnung $ Nähanleitungskizze Fux 1308

2 Blätter Blatt 1

linke H'fußnaht
·· V'fußabnäher
·· V'fußnaht
·· Rückensäumen

rechte V'fußnaht
·· V'fußabnäher
·· H'fußnaht
·· Rückensäum.

Ohren überwendling nähen

linke Schwanznaht

rechte Schwanznaht

Fig. 222 above: 'Fux 1308,02' from 1926 is made of red-brown mohair plush. Adorned with a large bell, rubber cord and ivory ring, it was made as hanging toy for prams.

Fig. 223 left: Part 1 of the 'laying and sewing instruction sketch' for the piece 'Fux 1308' from 1926.

Fig. 224 below: Part 2 of the 'laying and sewing instruction sketch' for the piece 'Fux 1308', including further details.

Fig. 221 left: A stamp from the prototype drawing department, 'Muzeibü', on the back of some instructions.

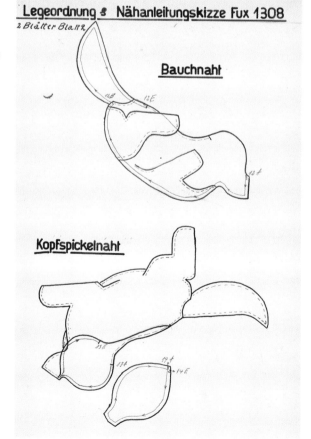

Legeordnung $ Nähanleitungskizze Fux 1308

2 Blätter Blatt 2

Bauchnaht

Kopfspickelnaht

During the next step all the individually cut and stamped parts that belong to a piece are joined together. Every Steiff animal is individually sewn together at a sewing machine. To prevent the seams being visible later from the outside, they are sewn from the inside. In trade jargon this is known as sewing 'inside out'. Extremely dextrous, nimble fingers are needed to ensure that the pile is always stroked into the seam during sewing, while still manoeuvring around the tightest curve. The speed and confidence with which the seamstresses work are really quite amazing. Today, as 100 years ago, nothing is left to chance. Every step is precisely planned and documented. To ensure that each and every seam is correctly placed, there are detailed laying and sewing instructions. To give an indication of the high standards, the work principles here are based on the same ones used in producing a valuable fur coat.

Fig. 225: A Steiff employee making one
of the voice mechanisms.

When all the individual parts have been sewn, they are turned the right way round: just like turning a sock the right way out, the mohair plush is turned to the outside. The smaller the individual part, naturally the more difficult it is to turn.

Today, the insides of the toy animals consist almost solely of synthetic stuffing materials that are washable and that remain hygienic in every circumstance. From 1950 until the turn of the millennium a pre-formed foam core was used to give soft bodies a stable shape. There are, however, numerous pieces that are stuffed with excelsior in the good old tradition. At the same time as they get their filling, Steiff animals also receive their voices. The voice mechanism is embedded in the middle of the body within the stuffing material so that no edges or corners can be seen or felt from the outside.

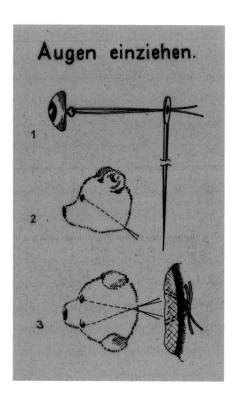

Fig. 226: Instruction from 1958 for attaching the eyes.

Fig. 227: The bear 'Bärle 80 PAB' from 1905. In this year cardboard discs were used to join the movable limbs to the body for the first time.

After stuffing, the individual parts are sewn together and the final seams that had remained open for the stuffing process are closed. Jointed animals with movable arms, legs and/or heads have firm cardboard discs at the points to be joined. Two interlocking discs that match up with each other are subsequently joined with a split pin. In this way, the movable joints of the individual limbs and head are joined to the body. This technique was first applied to the PAB 'Bärle' (roughly: 'cute little bear') series 100 years ago. PAB stands for 'Plüsch, angescheibt, beweglich' or 'plush, disk-jointed, movable'.

The stitching and exact positioning of its eyes are crucial in determining the final appearance of the Steiff animal. The mouth, nose and claws are stitched by hand, following the model. Even the eyes are applied by hand. Threads for glass eyes, for example, are led through the head, then pulled tight and knotted together at the back of the head. There are precise instructions for these steps as well. Then it's time for the finishing touches. Drawn features or shading are applied with the help of an airbrush pistol that works on air pressure. A great deal of experience, talent, a practised eye and a calm hand are necessary, for one wrong move with the fine paint spray can totally destroy all the work accomplished to that point. After the accessories – such as silk bows, clothing, collars, bells and so on – have been attached, the animal is once again checked extensively in the quality control department. If necessary, final adjustments are made. Any scraps of thread and material are picked from the fur. It's then given a good brush to remove any last bits of fluff.

Fig. 228: Quality certificate from the Bavarian District Court Factory Inspectorate (LGA) for Margarete Steiff GmbH.

Fig. 229: Certificate for 'Textiles tested for harmful substances according to Öko-Tex Standard 100'.

Before the piece finally receives its Steiff button, marking it unmistakably as a Steiff animal, it must undergo one last, strict test. Under the terms of a monitoring agreement, Steiff's entire toy collection is continually tested and monitored for safety, harmlessness to health, suitability for use and quality by the Bavarian District Court Factory Inspectorate (abbreviated to LGA in German). The LGA issues a quality certificate to prove this. In addition, all articles and products for babies from the category 'cosy friends' are checked by the International Group for Research and Testing in the Area of Textile Ecology (known, for short, in German as Öko-Tex) according to 'Standard 100'. This means they are continually tested, particularly for the presence of any harmful substances. With the declaration 'Textiles tested for harmful substances according to Öko-Tex Standard 100', Öko-Tex awards the product with a certificate attesting to the absence of substances harmful to people.

Then the time has come. The famous little button that has graced every Steiff animal since 1st November 1904 is applied to the left ear of the piece together with its ear tag. The 'Original Steiff' animal is ready – and with it one more product representing not just the tradition cultivated and maintained at Steiff for the past 125 years, but also the progress that has characterised the family-owned company's activities and ambitions for just as many years.

Fig. 230: This 2005 anniversary bear also embodies 125 years of tradition and progress by the family company, founded by Margarete Steiff in 1880.

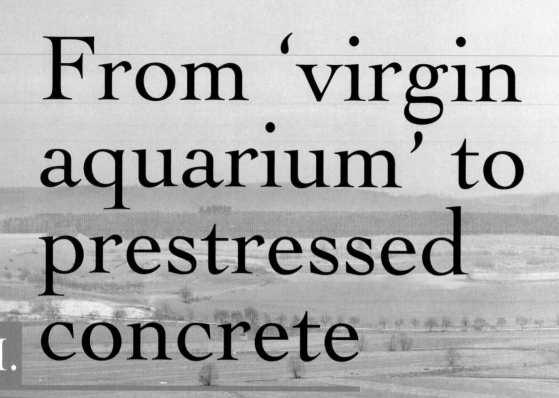

From 'virgin aquarium' to prestressed concrete

THE FAMOUS GLASS BUILDINGS AND OTHER

PRODUCTION BUILDINGS

Fig. 231: The offices at Mühlstraße in the foreground; behind it the new toy factory.

Fig. 232: Behind the construction site, the building Margarete Steiff used as her home on Mühlstraße can be clearly seen.

Margarete Steiff's parents earned their living with a construction company. Her brother Friedrich took over his father's company in 1888. And, during her brother's education to become a master builder, Margarete also showed a great deal of interest in this subject. For Friedrich's six sons, from their earliest childhood onwards, construction was a way of life thanks to their father's company. It is no wonder, therefore, that the family took on the planning and realisation of its own production buildings right from the beginning without a second thought.

This lack of concern, combined with the desire to build in the most cost-effective and efficient way possible, is certainly also one of the reasons why Margarete Steiff's company buildings were something special, both then and now. After the workshop in her parents' house on Lederstraße had become too small, she moved into the first building built especially for her, on Mühlstraße, in 1890. Barely a decade later, 1899-1900, this building needed the addition of an annex as the space available was just no longer sufficient. And the first 'glass building' had already been completed by 1903 – a building that is still the object of special interest and that still houses Margarete Steiff GmbH's headquarters. At the time, it was known locally as the 'virgin aquarium' because it was mainly unmarried young women who were employed there to make toys.

Still today, those entering this building feel immediately the enduring appeal of the architecture: a combination of a touch of nostalgia with modern technology. But why did the family choose this particular type of construction? And was Richard Steiff really the architect, as has hitherto been assumed but never proven? The first question is answered rather easily: the reasons for making the buildings from glass simply had more to do with practicality and their commercial use. Glass buildings had the advantage of being comparatively quick to build, their light rooms provided ideal conditions for the production of toys, they offered almost innumerable variations and possibilities for use, and the running costs were also extremely low.

Today the second question can also be answered without any doubt: Richard Steiff both planned and built this building. He travelled to London for the first time in 1897 where he visited the Crystal Palace, built in 1851 to house the Great Exhibi-

154

Fig. 233: In 1903 the east building was created, the first glass building used for Margarete Steiff's toy factory.

Fig. 234: The Crystal Palace was built in London in 1851 on the occasion of the Great Exhibition.

tion. And he visited Munich many times, a city whose glass palace was finished in 1854. It seems reasonable to assume that Richard was inspired to design the glass buildings in Giengen by his visits to the edifices in London and Munich.

Another piece of circumstantial evidence comes from the invitations to tender: enquiries regarding offers to build the east building were sent to the companies Eisenwerk München AG and Bauanstalt für Glashäuser in Charlottenburg. The conditions for the offers were very specific and detailed in form, measurements, foundations, and room divisions. So the two companies tendered comparable offers. This was only possible given the fact that a design was sent from Giengen.

Eisenwerk München AG ended up getting the contract on the basis of its preliminary design of 19th December 1902. On 28th January 1903, after reworking the design twice, an application to build was sent to the city. Any remaining doubts regarding the authorship of Richard Steiff have been completely eliminated by the following passages from two letters. The first letter was sent by Margarete Steiff to her nephew Paul in the US on 14th December 1902. She wrote the following of the glass building:

Fig. 235: Richard Steiff, the imaginative inventor of the Teddy bear, also designed the glass buildings for the toy factory.

Construction is now serious, we bought Öttingers' garden for 3,200, for the old women wouldn't sell for anything else. Richard envisages a building made of iron and glass, going straight across both gardens, 30/12 metres in one room, lower basement, ground and upper floor with high windows – whether it will work only time will tell. Will probably cost 40 thousand, but that can't be changed and it is something solid, and it seems to be practicable. Steam or warm water heating needs to be added as well. All the work will be done in this building ... Richard is writing to all kinds of suppliers, already has a very cheap offer in linoleum. Richard said that Franz would need to take over the supervision so that Richard can turn to producing prototypes and the catalogue.

Another passage from a recently discovered letter was sent by Richard Steiff from the US on 6th January 1931; this supports the evidence from the previous statements:

I myself have felt this way until now: 'we' bought this field; the 'year...' brought that building, then this innovation 'was' introduced, etc. But today I thank my lucky stars not only that I could think up and realise the fundamental decisions, but that they also 'coincidentally?' led me along the right path. ... As back then in Giengen, when, with my rubber boots and gloves on, I began throwing rocks into the meadow and laying down

the street to where the factory would be – just like the one I had imagined adding to the city building plan when I was an apprentice with the city's master builder in 1893, I started construction here [AUTHOR'S NOTE: IN THE US] *completely from scratch.*
I used the best possible pioneers for it. There's no other producer today can even touch our store front in New York, like our factory at home.

The east building put up in 1903 has quite often been a subject of study for building experts. The most recent analysis was undertaken in 1998 by Cornelia Denks, at the time a student in the faculty for architecture at the Technical University in Munich. Her findings, which follow, make a good starting-point for a discussion of the technical questions and the building's significance in architectural history. Denks concluded that the building is 'over-constructed':

Smaller sections, fewer vertical plates and fewer stiffening measures would have made the building seem more delicate. But at least the building was saved from any construction damage whatsoever. Built to a much higher specification for stability than strictly necessary, the design obviously prevented any sign of buckling or warping tension, which would have had disastrous effects on the full glass walls. It is a well-known fact that at Ahlfeld's Fagus Works, more than 40 panes jumped out of their frames.

For sure Richard's top priority regarding the building was not the visual design, contrary to Steiff animals. He wanted to build a suitable and safe building – and he achieved that. Denks' architectural analysis was especially interested in the façade:

It is not only the attractive appearance of this glass skin, but also the pioneering technical achievement that is so amazing. This is the first factory known to use only a double shell of glass as outer wall. Until then this method, intended as a heat protection as well as a shield for the construction, was only known as a design for roofs and hothouses. ... The delicate construction of the profiles and the regular mounting via sideplates mean that this can be regarded as a 'curtain façade'. The first 'curtain wall', celebrated as pioneering work and credited by architects as heralding the modern age, was part of San Francisco's Hallidie Building, not built until 1918. In THE ARCHITECT WALTER GROPIUS, Winifried Nerdinger refers to the Fagus Works as being the first curtain façade in Europe. This treatise contradicts that supposition, though it does not dispute the extra refinement of creating a fully transparent corner. Of course, Gropius was a better master of expressing technical innovations in architectural terms. Without an architect, clearly the Steiff design did not have a mouthpiece for publication. But it is equally clear that an inventive spirit on the fringes of public events can achieve a great deal.

These are well-chosen words: "without an architect, clearly the Steiff design did not have a mouthpiece for publication", and "of course, Gropius was a better master of expressing technical innovations in architectural terms." But in her architectural analysis Denks also revealed that "it is a well-known fact that, at Ahlfeld's Fagus Works, more than 40 panes jumped out of their frames".

157

The Fagus Works in Alfeld was, as we know, designed by Gropius in 1911 and it is still acknowledged as the first example of 'new building' in Germany. It is considered to be Gropius' attempt to unite pure building with art in an industrial building made of the new materials iron and glass. At any rate, Denks came to the following conclusion:

Steiff's east building is an example of a clever and objectively planned and executed engineering construction. Down to the smallest details, ideas were taken from all the most particular refinements of different styles (hothouse design, textile factory design etc.) from which a new system was developed that was worth using again and again for extensions. Since these transparent, modular, flexible construction hulls have also proved to be extremely durable – and durability is today a much-praised element of quality – I think that the frontier has clearly been moved from a 'soulless' practical building towards architectural art!

Until 1910 a few more of these glass buildings were put up on the Steiff site. The east building with an area of 1,080 m², which was erected in less than six months in 1903, had already been followed in 1904 by the west building with 6,840 m² of workspace and the north building in 1908 with another 6,120 m². The last glass buildings to be put up were in 1910 the carpentry building plus various extra rooms, which added up to a total of 1,080 m². Thus the entire working area of Steiff's glass buildings came to 15,120 m².

Fig. 236: The toy factory's glass buildings – a piece of modern industrial architecture.

158

In the winter a steam heating system was turned on to warm the buildings, the pipes of which could be turned on and off individually. In the summer months the buildings were whitewashed from the outside in order to avoid direct sunlight coming in, thus preventing overheating. There was only an imperceptible decrease in the availability of light. In the cooler months the white chalk colour could easily be washed off again with sponges. In 1903, 25 telephone extensions were already being prepared. In 1980 the building was protected by being given 'historical monument' status, for it was "a forerunner of the so-called 'anonymous avant-garde' ".

In 1923 Steiff started building again. This time, however, they did not use such a spectacular style of construction and the new buildings were erected in a conventional way. The two connecting bridges of the west and north buildings, the vault building on the north-east side of the north building, and the large Brenz bridge, which made direct access to the railway possible and once would become the main gate of the factory, all were created in reinforced concrete. In 1950 a one-storey building was created for the showpiece and belt drive department. A new three-storey building was put up to house toy production in 1953, this time in pre-stressed concrete, at that time a modern material.

So the outward appearance of the factory area and its buildings has been transformed many times over the past 125 years. And that will not change in the future. What will remain is the individual character lent to the whole area by its unmistakable glass buildings dating right from the beginning of the last century, corresponding excellently with the toy animals of Margarete Steiff GmbH – which are just as unmistakable.

Fig. 237: In the summer the glass façades were whitewashed from the outside in order to avoid direct sunlight and overheating.

Fig. 238: Margarete Steiff GmbH's factory
area changed its appearance many times
over the last 125 years (aerial view from
the 1980s).

VIII. The World of Steiff ...

... AND OTHER STEIFF

ACTIVITIES

Fig. 239: The new Steiff Museum welcomes
visitors with the sign 'The World of Steiff' since
June 2005.

Fig. 240: The house where Margarete Steiff was born at Lederstraße 26, seen here in 2004.

THE HOUSE WHERE
MARGARETE STEIFF WAS BORN

The building at Lederstraße 26 in Giengen was built in the mid-seventeenth century. In 1843 it came into the possession of master builder Friedrich Steiff, and four years later Margarete Steiff was born in the house. During a reconstruction in 1874, the first floor was provided with a proper workshop for a streamstress. In 1897 the Steiff family sold the building. In the ensuing years, it changed owners several times until it was finally bought in 2002 by Steiff Beteiligungsgesellschaft, which renovated it thoroughly.

The renovation gave the house where Margarete Steiff was born once again the appearance that it had around the year 1880. The rooms were lovingly restored to their original state as far as possible. With the aid of colour analyses it was possible to determine the paints used during that time, both inside and out. The wooden floors and tiling were replaced following historical examples, and the windows were rebuilt in line with the originals. The interior was decorated with furniture and accessories from the Biedermeier period. It has been possible to visit the 'Margarete Steiff's Birthplace' museum since November 2003.

Visitors are led through the building on a 'journey into the past' by numbered information boards. The visit begins in Margarete Steiff's workshop, where her old sewing machine and one of her wheelchairs can be viewed. The visit continues to the bedroom, bathroom, and finally to the living room with its cast-iron stove. There are several boards here, which give a short, illustrated description of the life of Margarete Steiff.

The kitchen area follows and contains an old stove and dishes from the mid-nineteenth century. A little porch and a staircase take visitors to the old kitchen gar-

Fig. 241: The entrance area of the house before and after renovations.

den and further along the corridor back to the attic and into Margarete's parents' bedroom, where Margarete Steiff came into the world. In the next room a series of pictures awaits. These show details of the individual steps of the restoration work; various other boards also give information about the history of the house. Stepping through a door, visitors come to a half-timbered attic, which is listed as an historical monument. The tour ends back on the ground floor, where early Steiff animals are exhibited in a number of glass showcases.

The house where Margarete Steiff was born was as good as forgotten for many years; thanks to the involvement of Steiff Beteiligungsgesellschaft mbH it has now become a historical jewel open to the general public.

Fig. 242: Logo of the Alligator Ventilfabrik on the 1922 catalogue.

The Alligator Valve Factory GmbH

In 1920 the Alligator Ventilfabrik (Alligator Valve Factory) was founded as a department within Margarete Steiff GmbH. Just one year later it was registered as an independent subsidiary. The company evolved from the previous 'Metall-dreherei', the metalworking department of Margarete Steiff GmbH. During World War I, in order to avoid having the company's metalworking machines confiscated by the military, army contracts were fulfilled there. After the end of the war, a practical use had to be found for the idle machines. At first, until mid-1919, bare iron screws were produced there. But the technical interest of the Steiff brothers very soon steered the department's attention to tube type tyre valves made of brass. This development at the beginning of the 1920s was described in the anniversary publication of 1930 as follows:

Fig. 243: Cover of the Alligator catalogue from 1924.

Fig. 244: "The proven Steiff lighter usable for years and the cheapest pocket lighter," states the Alligator catalogue of 1924.

Steiff now turned to making tube type tyre valves. In the ensuing years 1920-1923, under the direction of Mr Richard Steiff, works manager Johannes Reichhardt created the range of machines necessary for rationalised, modern production of valves. Working restlessly, he invented and built machines, rebuilt old machines, and purchased the most modern automated machines. ... From 1920 onward the accounting was kept separately from Steiff's main business, and the department was placed on its own two feet. In 1921 the department received its own company name: Alligator Ventil-fabrik Giengen a.d. Brenz. ... After Mr Richard Steiff had left for the US, Mr Otto Steiff took over the Alligator department as the responsible managing director on the main company's behalf.

The catalogue from 1924 contained, alongside bike valves, products such as 'car pump nipples', 'car valve plugs', 'jointed double plugs' and many more. There was even a Steiff cigarette lighter in the range.

Most of the products were based on the company's own inventions and these soon made Alligator known all over the world. The business extended into making valves for cars and motorbikes. From the most modest beginnings, this company had developed into an industry leader. Right up to the present day, Alligator still designs and produces valves for all types of vehicles, from wheelbarrows, bicycles and cars to valves for heavy digging machines.

166

Alligator's product range also includes the entire spectrum of valve accessories, the manufacture of all types of tyre-filling apparatuses, and industrial valves that are used in fire extinguishers, tank constructions and air conditioning systems. About half the production is sold through worldwide export, and almost 170 million pieces of the main product – car tyre valves – are manufactured annually in the main Giengen factory and in another workshop in Mülheim am Main. It is said, by the way, that the name 'Alligator' was chosen because the good grip of the valve surface was similar to the scaly skin of the reptile of the same name.

Fig. 245: Logo of the Steiff Förder- und Automatisierungstechnik GmbH.

Steiff Förder- und Automatisierungstechnik GmbH

In 1927 an independent belt department was created within the house of Steiff. It was based on the invention of the so-called 'spiral belt' technology, in which Ernst Steiff, the youngest nephew of Margarete, also had a share. This is a special process to manufacture an endless, seamless drive belt. This special belt has the advantage of not having a terminal patch, which can lead to imbalance and knocks in fast-running machines and engines. Based on this special knowledge, a department to manufacture this seamless belt was established within the toy factory. Over the years both the products and their manufacturing processes were continually improved technically.

At the beginning of the 1970s varying band and belt drive materials and their manufacture were added to the programme, which meant that the belts were especially made to fit certain uses (for example, soldering studs onto them, joining them seamlessly, making rims, etc.). At the same time, the company was also beginning to produce entire conveyor belt facilities, upon which the seamless belts could be used. At first the conveyor belts were built under license according to a modular unit construction system. Little by little Steiff's own system was created from this, chiefly made of aluminium profiles. Since 1978 the former department belonging to Margarete Steiff GmbH has been managed as an independent company.

Steiff Förder- und Automatisierungstechnik GmbH, with around 60 employees, is able to produce and install even complex industrial facilities with the most modern programmable controllers or computer controls. At a small scale the belt- and band-weaving department still remains and today continues to manufacture seamlessly woven products for very specialised uses.

Fig. 246: Conveyor belt technology by Steiff.

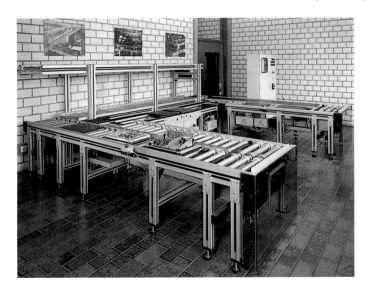

167

Fig. 247 above left: Steiff showpiece in the foyer of American wholesaler Geo Borgfeld & Co., New York.

Fig. 248 above: Mickey Mouse, the world-famous cartoon character by Walt Disney, was a special Steiff article for the American market from 1931.

STEIFF USA

Already during Margarete Steiff's lifetime, the company was maintaining good contacts with the US. Paul Steiff stayed there for almost two years at the beginning of the last century, laying the cornerstone for the company's success in sales there. Franz Steiff represented the company in 1904 at the World's Fair in St Louis. And even Richard Steiff, who emigrated to the US in 1923, made trips across the Atlantic before 1912. In 1912 Otto Steiff travelled to the US and completed the establishment of the subsidiary Margarete Steiff & Co., Inc. in New York, a project most likely begun by Richard Steiff. Twelve months later Geo Borgfeld & Co., New York, took over the exclusive distribution rights and kept them, with some interruptions caused by World War I, until the temporary end of American business ties in the mid-1930s.

After World War II, Reeves International, Inc. in New Jersey was awarded the exclusive distribution rights for Steiff in the US. This arrangement continued until finally on 1st January 1992 – 80 years after the founding of the first Steiff sub-

Fig. 249: Bald eagle – a limited edition of 1,500 pieces from 2003 for Steiff USA.

sidiary in the US – again an own marketing and distribution company was created, Steiff USA, LP. The registered address was 'Toy Center', the epicentre of the American toy industry on Fifth Avenue in New York. There the firm resided until May 2000. Then came the move to Raynham in Massachusetts, where a building of 2,800 m^2 was waiting for them, in the middle of a generously laid-out office complex. This removed the problem of the geographic separation of office and warehouse that had been prevalent until that point, making more efficient working possible.

Already since the 1920s more and more products were being made especially for the American market. Mickey and Minnie Mouse, as well as the cartoon cat Felix, were just a few prominent examples.

Since the introduction of the limited collector's editions in 1980, there have regularly also been special editions made exclusively for North America. Making the right decision in choosing these special products – mostly limited editions – has been one of Steiff USA's tasks since 1992.

Fig. 250: The current logo of the Steiff Club.

THE STEIFF CLUB

The Steiff Club, founded in April 1992, has created a forum for enthusiasts and collectors of old and new creations with the 'Button in Ear'. In its foundation year, 13,000 applications to join were accepted, and now the club has more than 55,000 members worldwide.

The introductory gift – a 7 cm tall mohair bear not available in any store – and the annual, exclusive limited club editions are in themselves already attractive arguments for signing up to the Steiff Club. For fans, however, it's the regular information right from the source that is so important: four times a year the informative and always up-to-date Club Magazine comes out. Other advantages of membership include the mailing of the complete Steiff catalogue and of informative and interesting brochures.

A lot is also done for the community spirit. In co-operation with the regional club dealers, regular club events are organised; these have both an informative and a social nature. Group trips are also offered from time to time; these have led as far as the US in the past. And, last but not least, there is the trading zone. This is where members have the opportunity to publish free ads, either in printed form or on the Internet, to reach large amounts of people sharing the same hobby and/or passion.

It is obvious that the Steiff Club is popular: its continually increasing numbers prove this. Numerous letters from readers containing praise, critiques, wishes – often also accompanied by personal photos of much-loved Steiff animals – prove how highly the club is thought of. The reasons behind the passion for collecting vary, but regardless everyone finds a forum here, from those enthusiasts and fans more driven by an emotional attraction to the Steiff brand to professional collectors.

In the anniversary year a very special highlight is waiting for all club members. The 'old villa', where the club headquarters is located, is being renovated and a 'club lounge' is being created on the ground floor of the building. From the middle of 2005 the Steiff Club can welcome its members there. In addition to being able to view an exhibition of the exclusive club editions, they get information about club activities here, may have a chat, and see what's going on.

THE STEIFF GALLERIES

The toy market has changed a great deal in the last few years. Many toy shops, often including very established ones, have disappeared from city centres and their pedestrian zones. Contrary to this trend, interest in Steiff products has increased and demand grown. In reality, it is no longer only children's hearts that Steiff animals are conquering these days; adults are fulfilling their own childhood wishes as well. Thus, the popular toy animal with the famous 'Button in Ear' has become a sought-after gift for young and old alike.

Since Margarete Steiff GmbH's distribution policy has always concentrated on retail trade, these changes in the market have demanded new ways of thinking. In order to serve all its target groups adequately, Margarete Steiff GmbH has developed its own franchising system, the Steiff Gallery. Both the location and the tasteful furnishings are part of the carefully chosen and harmonious design, presenting the Steiff brand in a suitably dignified way. Selected shop locations, chosen using location analyses, the new style of shop design, the beautiful, constantly updated décor, and last but not least excellent franchise partners as dealers lend an exclusive atmosphere. The pleasing appearance of the Steiff galleries appeals to all ages. A marketing campaign designed especially for the galleries, together with targeted regional and national advertising, have guaranteed great success thus far.

In 1997 the first Steiff Gallery was opened in Hamburg. Since then, more of these shops have opened in Berlin, Bremen, Düsseldorf, Hamburg, Hanover, Kiel, London, Munich, Nuremberg, Stuttgart, Tokyo, Vienna, Wiesbaden and Zurich.

The joint marketing of the Steiff Galleries has been supported since 2000 by an annually issued, exclusive and limited edition special product, the 'Gallery Bear'. Eight years after its debut, the introduction of the Steiff Galleries can, without exaggeration, be said to be a most successful implementation of a new business concept.

Fig. 251: The reproductions of 'Richard Steiff's Bear' from 1905 and the 'Camel on Pincushion' from 1904 are available exclusively for members as the club editions of 2005, either in a set or individually.

Fig. 252: Every year a limited 'Gallery Bear' is made exclusively for the Steiff Galleries. The bear for 2000 was issued in a limited edition of 2,000 pieces.

Fig. 253: The Steiff Galleries – here the
attractive store in Wiesbaden – are beautifully
eye-catching, enhancing pedestrian zones and
exclusive shopping streets.

Fig. 254: The new museum of experience, 'The World of Steiff', was finished just in time for the 125th anniversary and looks like a monumental Steiff button.

THE WORLD OF STEIFF

In keeping with the tradition of Richard Steiff, who had given the factory grounds their unmistakable character between 1903 and 1910 with his groundbreaking glass buildings, a new building was erected for 'The World of Steiff' in 2004-2005 – an example of modern and courageous architecture, designed by the Zurich architect Andreas Ramseier.

Exactly 25 years after the first Steiff Museum was opened on the lower level of the 1903 east building, and just in time for the company's 125th anniversary, this fascinating museum of experience for young and old will be open to the public for the first time. Visitors will be fascinated by the world of experience on three levels, a total of 2,400 m² of exhibitions. The museum displays Steiff animals and 125 years of continuous company history. There is a lot to see, hear and, of course, to feel.

After entering the foyer, bear paws on the floor show the way through the new museum. From the foyer, the tour goes to Margarete Steiff's sewing studio. There the founder herself explains how the first Steiff animal – the 'Elefäntle' – was created. After that the tour leads to Richard Steiff's ideas laboratory. Here, in an authentic replica of the 'Muzeibü', a Teddy bear comes alive to tell stories of his brilliant inventor's creations.

From there, visitors continue on, together with the Teddy bear and its friend Lea, into an animated fantasy world. Looking down from the gallery, visitors are offered a view into Steiff City's past and present; looking up gives a view into the stuffed animals' future. Like a museum, Steiff City presents the story of 125 years of toy production, in all its variety, separating the narrative into themed areas. The most valuable pieces are shown in special glass showcases. And a visit to the production display very clearly demonstrates the individual work processes that go into the beautiful animals.

A cosy play corner has been added for big and small alike. And, for those who would like to take a Steiff animal home after the tour, there is a large assortment of products available in the museum shop. Children and adults who might be hungry or thirsty after this exciting museum experience can go to the café, waiting with 80 seats inside and out and a large menu.

Fig. 255: Richard Steiff's Teddy bear with one
of the early examples of the famous first Steiff
animal, the 'Elefäntle'. Both can be admired in
the new museum.

Appendix

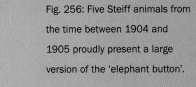

Fig. 256: Five Steiff animals from the time between 1904 and 1905 proudly present a large version of the 'elephant button'.

Steiff's product numbering system from 1905

With the introduction of 'Bärle PAB' ('Little Bear', PAB stands for Plüsch-angescheibt-beweglich or plush, jointed, movable) in 1905, Steiff also introduced its new product numbering system – only replaced by a more modern method in 1968. With the aid of a 'talking' number system it became possible to catalogue the numerous products and clearly identify each one by using the number descriptions. Article numbers are used in Steiff's catalogues and are additionally printed on each of the Steiff products' ear tags.

Each individual digit of the four-digit number has its own meaning, describing both material and composition of each product. The new product number of 'Little Bear 35 PAB' is now '5335,1'. Using this animal as an example, the system is explained as follows.

The 5 placed at the beginning gives information about the style of the bear: in our example, it is jointed. The second digit – the 3 – describes the material used; this product is made of mohair. The third and fourth digits, 3 and 5, reveal the size of the product: 35 cm. Since measurements are taken in a sitting position for jointed bears, the sitting 'Little Bear 35 PAB' measures 35 cm.

The numbers and letters placed after the comma mainly stand for accessory details.

The 1 in our example means that it is a stuffed product. The number after the comma is also sometimes used to mark the difference between variations in clothing on a type of animal. In the 1930s, for example, a bear wearing clothes by the name of 'Puppbär' ('Doll Bear') was included in the Steiff range. It was offered in eleven different versions, numbered from 1 to 11. The numbers each stood for the varying outfits as part of the overall product number after the comma. If a product number does not contain a comma, letters such as br, c, g and w could be used to differentiate the colours brown, caramel, gold and white. The letters M and B denote female and male (Maid and Bub). In order to avoid mixing up the types of animals, for with the very same product number we could also be talking about a jointed, stuffed, 35 cm tall elephant made of mohair for example, Steiff put another two- or, in a few cases, a three-digit number in front of the product number. This is the 'series number'. Bears, for example, carry the series number 12, elephants the number 20. The series number is rarely printed onto the ear tag, but it is always included in the catalogues.

The most frequent and important numbers are listed below:

1. First digit – style:

    1 = standing

    2 = lying

    3 = sitting

    4 = begging / sitting up / standing on
       back legs

    5 = jointed

    6 = young

    7 = caricatured

    8 = ball-jointed neck

    9 = with clock-work mechanism

2. Second digit – type of material:

    1 = felt

    2 = short-pile plush / coat plush

    3 = mohair

    4 = velvet

    5 = lamb's wool plush / wool plush

    6 = cellulose/artificial silk
       plush/Dralon plush

    7 = cotton fabric / oil cloth

    8 = wood

    9 = fur/metal

Third and fourth digits – size in cm, for example:

    10 = 10 cm

    17 = 17 cm

    35 = 35 cm etc.

Number after the comma – accessories:

    0 = without wheels

    1 = soft stuffing / also: squeaker
       (speaks when pressed)

    2 = automatic voice (growler) /
       double squeaker /
       cord-activated voice

    3 = music-box

    4 = simplified

    5 = removable saddle

    6 = tails / clothing

    7 = muzzle/backpack

    8 = steering apparatus

    9 = removable rocker

    b = hot-water bottle

    ex = eccentric wheels

    H = neck mechanism /
       tail turns head

    ST = steering

Licence for registered pattern – translation

County Court Heidenheim

the 25th of May, 1903.

It is herewith certified
(...) that in the
(...)
(...) registry of patterns

Band I – page 65

under Number 1

on 3rd June 1899 the following was registered:

Company: Margarete Steiff in Giengen/Br.

Registered: 3rd June 1899, 5:30 in the evening

Pattern: a sealed package with 3 drawings
and 23 original patterns of stuffed
toys with material coverings:
nos. 207., 424., 459., 462, 468., 533, 535, 536.,
549, 550, 548, 555, 581., 591b 591f 591g
591i 605, 6062m. 606m 601m 643, 715,
716, 1241, 42 and 43. 461.

three-dimensional creations

Protected: 3 years

Reg. in bus. reg.   (stamp)   Clerk of the Court:
1903 (signature)   K. Württ. County Court   (signature)

K. Amtsgericht _Heidenheim._

den *25*ten *Mai* 19*03*

~~Auf Anordnung des Königlichen Amtsgerichts werden Sie benachrichtigt~~, daß in dem

~~Handelsregister,~~ ~~Abth. für Einzelfirmen~~ ~~Genossenschaftsregister~~ ~~Vereinsregister~~
~~Abth. für Gesellschaftsfirmen~~

~~Güterrechtsregister~~ — Musterregister —

Band *I.* Blatt — Seite *65*

unter der Nummer *1*

am *3. Juni* 18*99* Folgendes eingetragen worden ist:

Firma: Margarete Steiff in Giengen a/b.

Anmeldung: 3. Juni 1899, Abends 5½ Uhr.

Muster: [handwritten, partly illegible]

Nr. 207, 424, 459, 462, 468, 533, 535, 536,
549, 550, 548, 555, 581, 591², 591⁴, 591⁵,
591⁶, 605, 606²ᵐ, 606ᵐ, 601ᵐ, 643, 715,
716, 1241, 42 u 43, 461.

Schutzfrist: 3 Jahren.

Gerichtsschreiber:

The creation of the teddy bear

1901   Shiny plush, today's mohair plush, was first offered in the Steiff catalogue and only for the 50 cm bear on wheels in the colours brown, white and grey.

1902   Development by Richard Steiff of the first jointed bear prototype made of shiny plush under the product description 'Bear 55 PB' (PB stands for plush and movable). One of these bears was sent by ship to the US as a sales sample.

1903   Paul Steiff offered the bear to his American customers, and in Germany '55 PB' was officially presented for the first time at the spring fair in Leipzig. The first picture of it was found in the catalogue of new products for the year 1903. On 13th July 'Bear 55 PB' was registered at the County Court in Heidenheim. Sales numbers were not recorded.

1904   In the Steiff catalogue from 1st February only 'Bear 55 PB' continued to be offered. On 5th March, 'Bear 35 PB' was registered at the County Court in Heidenheim. During the entire year, 12,000 Steiff bears were manufactured. How many of which type is not known. „Toys with movable joints attached with a two-part wire and whose closing elements lie inside the trunk of the object" are registered.

1905   On 15th February the application to register 'Little Bear 35 PAB' ('Bärle', PAB stands for plush – disk-jointed – movable) was handed in. Its appearance was similar to the famous modern-day teddy bear. The pattern registration, for a „shaft or pole with projections pressed from the perimeter to hold objects pushed onto it", was applied for on 8th June. The bears offered in the Steiff catalogue of 15th August comprised the following jointed types:
1. The new model, called 'Little Bear PAB' in seven sitting sizes: 17, 22, 28, 35, 43, 50 and 80 cm, and in three different colours: light brown, dark brown and white. The product numbers additionally introduced were 5317,1 and 5380,1.
2. The previous bear models known as '28' and '35 PB' (new product numbers 5328 and 5335).
   Details regarding production numbers from this year are not available.

1906   'Little Bear PB' was taken out of the Steiff range. Two further sizes of the new teddy bear were offered with the product numbers 5315 and 5325. The production of jointed bears numbered 385,393 in this year.

1907 The record year for bear production: a total of almost one million bears were sold by Margarete Steiff GmbH.

1908 More different-sized Teddy bears were added to the range. Additionally, the bear was now available with a 'growler' voice. Bear production numbered only 290,157 pieces, and sales sunk to 222,455 – a decrease due to the US economic crisis. In Europe, 'Teddy' was also beginning to establish himself, and so Teddy bear production continued at full capacity. Even if the legendary production numbers from 1907 were not going to be achieved, the worldwide success of the Teddy bear could no longer be halted.

Fig. 257:
'Bear 55 PB' as it was shown in the catalogue of 1903-1904.

Fig. 258: Margarete Steiff's grave, photographed on her 100th birthday in 1947.

The words on the grave of
Apollonia Margarete Steiff in Giengen a. Br.

Born in Giengen a. Br. on 24 July 1847
Died in Giengen a. Br. on 9 May 1909
Buried at the same 12 May 1909

Stpf. Siegle

funereal text: 2 Corinthians 12:9:

„My grace is sufficient for thee:
for my strength is made perfect in weakness."

Amen.

Eulogy given at Margarete Steiff's interment

Dear mourners so loved by Jesus Christ!

What should we say at this grave? I find it hard to find the words that match the meaning of this hour for us, to do justice to the size and depth of the loss that we all, all have suffered. How dear was the departed to each and every one of us without exception? There is first of all her family, who rose up in the world in such a short time, and who basically owe everything to her! There is the numerous host of employees who have lost not a master, but a mother. There are the many workers to whom she gave bread and work, the work certainly neither too great nor too arduous. There are above all the many weak, fragile, poor and needy people whom she took in with special love, to whom she gave an existence or for whom, at least, she lessened their need. You all cry at this grave. And I say: Yes, cry, cry! A 'Gretle Steiff' won't come along again very soon. The black flag waves outside with justice. It is as if it wants to say to us: the business didn't only lose its head, its clear and commanding spirit, it lost much more, even its heart, that was tangible in everything and through everything. God the father will sort out our Giengen. He takes our best, one after another. And he has now taken from us one of the very best.

Like a miracle she appeared before our eyes. We live in a time when people are of the opinion: God doesn't work miracles anymore. And all the time we had our dearly departed in front of our eyes as a new living miracle. For is it not a miracle when in her childhood she was such a poor, weak, fragile and helpless soul, of whom it was asked, with great concern: how will she manage? How will she get through? In her later life she cared for thousands of others, helped thousands of others, and became not only the recognised head of her family, but also the founder and director of a company active throughout the entire world. Is it not a miracle when one such person who during her childhood garnered only looks of sympathy, who was destined for an existence of little renown, quiet and almost forgotten, moves out into the public light, making a much loved and respected name for herself and her hometown in the surrounding areas and even across the wide ocean? That hasn't happened for centuries. And this is why the still grave around which we are gathered today calls out to us unbelievers: „Oh, you sceptics!" And it reminds us that the following remains true today: „It is God who has always performed the miracles, He who can bring us down and – up!" – „What is weak in the world God has chosen to make disgraced, that no one sings its praises!" – „My grace is sufficient for thee: for my strength is made perfect in weakness."

Yes, „My grace is sufficient for thee!" That is what she had to learn in her life, our departed. It happened to her as it did to the apostle, who had done his life's work under many terrible circumstances – and begged God the father three times to remove the trial from him. But the father gave him as an answer: „My grace is sufficient for thee!" Yes, that is also the way it was for her, whom we are mourning today, in her entire earthly course of life from the beginning until the last suffering, when the father took everything from her, even her natural courage and her sense of cheerfulness, where He left her completely helpless and left her only one thing – his grace and his compassion! Yes, she needed to learn that His grace was enough!

But praise be to God! And that is the second miracle, the greatest that He worked in this life, with the assistance of God she did learn this. It was not easy for her, for to find oneself in that situation is the hardest thing of all for a person's heart. It cannot come to an end without an inner struggle, without quiet tears that no one sees, without serious questioning, which cannot be answered by people alone. And believe you me, even our dearly departed knew of the struggles and tears. But praise be to God! The father helped her through, helped her to overcome these struggles. She learned that it was enough. She herself, in those days which – it is said – people can hardly bear, when the despondent human heart likes to become defiant and arrogant and self-willed and egoistic and domineering and ungrateful – she remained modest, simple, and humble as in the days before her fame. Her heart did not make something out of itself then, did not feel its own power then, did not praise its own humour and spirit, but met, with thanks, whatever the will of God threw into its lap. And how undemanding it remained of the people that surrounded it and of the pleasures of life; living simply even in the days of radiance and wealth; only when her heart wanted to give pleasure to others, do good for others, sacrifice itself for others, did she not stint; her word was that which God the father once said to Mary in Bethany: „She did what she could."

Enough, yes, and enough of God's grace! How important was the word 'grace' to her! Her soul hungered for this word, she founded her life on this word, all that she became during the course of her life was rooted in this word. The way she valued this word was an example to us all, how she, the busy one, visited the weak during those last years of insomnia, always finding time to come back to this word and from this word finding comfort, vitality and peace. And didn't she find it there? It was in the end the secret of this wonderful, rich, blessed life that she was fulfilled by grace.

Limitation shows the master, and those who limit themselves to the grace of God, concentrating on it, will become the master of all that is great and good and rich in blessing; he, the weak little plant, will be able to unfold his talents very differently in the honour of God, to heal, to the grateful joy of his fellow human beings. Yes, even more, those who acknowledge grace thankfully will receive not only a rich, blessed life, it will remain with them in times of suffering and death. It is wonderful how our dearly departed, even though some things were kept from her, despite the fact that she suffered long from insomnia during the last years of her life, wasn't morose, tired or dull, but had a strong, patient and consistent will and a happy nature. What is true of suffering is also true of dying. The waters are deeper there, the way darker, energy disappears completely; but especially when all vitality is broken completely, swallowed up by the weakness of dying, then the word lights up strongly and clear: „My grace is sufficient for thee: for my strength is made perfect in weakness."

Amen.

184

Buttons, ear tags and chest tags

Steiff's 'elephant button' led the way to the introduction of the trademark 'Button in Ear' in 1904. The tags attached to the products until then were paper tags, easy to remove. One year later the trademark was complemented by an additional tag that bore information regarding the product. In the mid-1920s another form of identification was introduced along with a neck tag that was attached to Steiff animals: the chest tag.

All three tags – button, ear tag and chest tag – have changed again and again in the last decades or have been replaced. For today's collector they are of extreme importance both for identification purposes and to estimate age. Attaching the trademarks served to retain company interests – of course they weren't necessarily thinking about potential future collectors. For this reason remnant supplies of buttons or tags were always used up, even if new models were already prepared. This is why, time and again, labels are found on some Steiff animals that don't correspond with the details found in the following list. Steiff buttons that undoubtedly originated in the 1930s can, for

example, be found on products that were clearly made in the period following World War II, marked by the presence of a US zone tag. In order to judge these special cases beyond doubt, one certainly needs a good deal of experience that can only be attained by an intense interest in collecting – when one is unsure, it is better to get advice from an expert.

By the way, only the button has been used since the beginning (the only exception being cheap products from the 1930s). For a long time the ear tag was left off and was only consistently used from the middle of the 1920s.

Of course, there have always been Steiff creations of every period that needed to be furnished with special markings because of their size or finishing. These include, for example, the small wool miniatures, wooden toys, cars and the large studio animals.

The following list describes the most important emblems and gives information about the periods when they were used.

1897 to 1904: Various tags, all showing the elephant whose trunk builds the 'S' from the abbreviation 'M.St.' (for Margarete Steiff), that were attached to the animals' bodies.

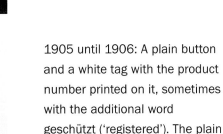

Fig. 259-262

From 1st November 1904 until 1905: The elephant button was used.

1905 until 1906: A plain button and a white tag with the product number printed on it, sometimes with the additional word geschützt ('registered'). The plain button was only used until 1906, but the illustrated tag was used until 1908.

1906 until 1924: Button with the word 'Steiff' in block letters. The second 'f' in Steiff is stylised with a long sweeping tail. The white tag contains the words 'Steiff Original'.

1923 to 1926: Button like the previous one, white tag with the product number and the words 'Steiff Original geschützt' and 'Germany Importé d'Allemagne' ('imported from Germany', in French) printed on it.

1926 to 1934: Button like the previous two, red tag with the product number and the words 'Steiff Original geschützt' and 'Made in Germany' printed on it.

1934 to 1943: Button like the previous three, yellow tag with printed elements like the red one, but sometimes in the abbreviated version 'Steiff Orig. gesch.'.

1936 to 1950: Button with shorter sweeping of the second 'f' in Steiff, tag as the previous one.

1946 to 1950: Plain button, also painted blue; light yellow or white tag made of paper at first and later of linen with the product number and the words 'Steiff Original geschützt' and 'Made in Germany' printed on it.

1947 to 1952: Button with 'Steiff' on it in large block letters without the sweeping 'f'. Tag like the previous one.

1947 to 1953: US zone tag, which was attached to the body, mostly sewn into a seam on the right arm or leg. This was a required designation of origin after World War II.

1952 to 1969: Button with the word Steiff in script, yellow tag with product number, Steiff logo – like on the button – In block letters and various other alternating words printed on it as follows: 'Steiff Original' or 'Original Steiff', 'Made in Germany', and 'Preis – Price', from 1950 also with material information on the back.

1969 to 1978: Rivet with embossed Steiff logo, yellow tag with product number and the world 'Original Steiff' and 'Made in Germany' printed on it. 'Preis' was left off, but the space used for the printed product number is a little larger. This tag was used until 1980.

1978 to 2000: Two-piece brass button with embossed 'Steiff' logo.

1978 to 1980: A gold-coloured button equal to the one with Steiff in script used in the 1950s and '60s was used at the same time as the two-piece brass button.

Fig. 270-274

Fig. 263-269

1993 to 2003: Special chest tag for all 'Classic' products.

From 2005: All 'Classic' products receive a chest tag with elephant logo and its own name.

From 2004: Every product receives a chest tag according to its category: 'classic', 'family', '... more', 'junior', and 'cosy friends'.

Fig. 296-301

There remain a number of other chest tag variations. These are used to denote club, collector and industry products.

The following Steiff emblems must also be mentioned:

1921 to 1927: A red or blue tag like this one was attached to the Steiff Schlopsnies dolls.

From 1984: The two-piece brass button, but without the 'Steiff' logo, was used to mark irregular products. The fastening piece on the back of this one also changed in 2000.

Fig. 302-304

Index

Photograph sources

Bechtle, Götz: 15

Ehrlinger, Barbara: 143

Eisenmann, Sibylle: 152

GAF Günther Pfeiffer GmbH: 6, 8, 12, 17-19, 23, 26, 32, 33, 35-41, 43, 75, 76, 89-94,
101, 120, 135, 155, 167, 172, 173, 178-179, 181, 183, 204-210, 213-215, 218, 220,
222, 240, 244, 248, 252, 253, 255, 256, 259-286, 288-299, 301, 303, 304

Heimat- und Altertumsverein, Geislingen/Steige: 10

Margarete Steiff GmbH: opening credits, table of contents, 2-5, 7, 9, 13, 14, 16, 20, 21,
24, 27, 29, 42, 44-74, 77-88, 95-100, 102-119, 121-134, 136-142, 144-151, 153-154,
156-164, 166, 168-170, 174-177, 180, 182, 184-203, 211, 212, 216, 217, 219, 221,
223-233, 235-239, 241-243, 245-247, 249-251, 254, 257, 258, 287, 300, 302,
appendix registration of pattern

Museum of the City of Giengen an der Brenz: 11

Neubrand, Otto; City Hall of the City of Giengen an der Brenz: 1

Photo archive www.360-berlin.de: 234

State Museum of Berlin, art library: 30, 31, 34

Steiff, Friedhelm: 165

Unknown sources: 22, 25, 28

Wöhrle, Paula: 171

Acknowledgements

At this point, also on behalf of Margarete Steiff GmbH, I would like to heartily thank everyone who helped in creating this book.

A special thank you to Gabriele Schöning, Manuela Fustig and Bernd Schmeizl, who stood by my side in the archives of Margarete Steiff GmbH during the research phase and who, with their funds of knowledge, were a huge help all the way to the printing phase of this book. Of course, this also applies to all the other Steiff employees who in some way, shape or form worked on this project.

I would like to thank my editor Marcus Reckewitz for his professional and co-operative collaboration. During the time spent together on this book I appreciated his loyal, unselfish and always competent support.

And, last but not least, I would like to thank my own team. These people relieved my load during the creation of this book, taking on routine activities and giving me the opportunity to concentrate fully on the task at hand. Their help, which went way beyond the call of duty, contributed greatly to the successful completion of this book.

Günther Pfeiffer